C-1472　　CAREER EXAMINATION SERIES

This is your
PASSBOOK for...

Senior Bridge & Tunnel Maintainer

Test Preparation Study Guide
Questions & Answers

NATIONAL LEARNING CORPORATION®

COPYRIGHT NOTICE

This book is SOLELY intended for, is sold ONLY to, and its use is RESTRICTED to individual, bona fide applicants or candidates who qualify by virtue of having seriously filed applications for appropriate license, certificate, professional and/or promotional advancement, higher school matriculation, scholarship, or other legitimate requirements of education and/or governmental authorities.

This book is NOT intended for use, class instruction, tutoring, training, duplication, copying, reprinting, excerption, or adaptation, etc., by:

1) Other publishers
2) Proprietors and/or Instructors of "Coaching" and/or Preparatory Courses
3) Personnel and/or Training Divisions of commercial, industrial, and governmental organizations
4) Schools, colleges, or universities and/or their departments and staffs, including teachers and other personnel
5) Testing Agencies or Bureaus
6) Study groups which seek by the purchase of a single volume to copy and/or duplicate and/or adapt this material for use by the group as a whole without having purchased individual volumes for each of the members of the group
7) Et al.

Such persons would be in violation of appropriate Federal and State statutes.

PROVISION OF LICENSING AGREEMENTS – Recognized educational, commercial, industrial, and governmental institutions and organizations, and others legitimately engaged in educational pursuits, including training, testing, and measurement activities, may address request for a licensing agreement to the copyright owners, who will determine whether, and under what conditions, including fees and charges, the materials in this book may be used them. In other words, a licensing facility exists for the legitimate use of the material in this book on other than an individual basis. However, it is asseverated and affirmed here that the material in this book CANNOT be used without the receipt of the express permission of such a licensing agreement from the Publishers. Inquiries re licensing should be addressed to the company, attention rights and permissions department.

All rights reserved, including the right of reproduction in whole or in part, in any form or by any means, electronic or mechanical, including photocopying, recording, or by any information storage and retrieval system, without permission in writing from the Publisher.

Copyright © 2025 by
National Learning Corporation

212 Michael Drive, Syosset, NY 11791
(516) 921-8888 • www.passbooks.com
E-mail: info@passbooks.com

PASSBOOK® SERIES

THE *PASSBOOK® SERIES* has been created to prepare applicants and candidates for the ultimate academic battlefield – the examination room.

At some time in our lives, each and every one of us may be required to take an examination – for validation, matriculation, admission, qualification, registration, certification, or licensure.

Based on the assumption that every applicant or candidate has met the basic formal educational standards, has taken the required number of courses, and read the necessary texts, the *PASSBOOK® SERIES* furnishes the one special preparation which may assure passing with confidence, instead of failing with insecurity. Examination questions – together with answers – are furnished as the basic vehicle for study so that the mysteries of the examination and its compounding difficulties may be eliminated or diminished by a sure method.

This book is meant to help you pass your examination provided that you qualify and are serious in your objective.

The entire field is reviewed through the huge store of content information which is succinctly presented through a provocative and challenging approach – the question-and-answer method.

A climate of success is established by furnishing the correct answers at the end of each test.

You soon learn to recognize types of questions, forms of questions, and patterns of questioning. You may even begin to anticipate expected outcomes.

You perceive that many questions are repeated or adapted so that you can gain acute insights, which may enable you to score many sure points.

You learn how to confront new questions, or types of questions, and to attack them confidently and work out the correct answers.

You note objectives and emphases, and recognize pitfalls and dangers, so that you may make positive educational adjustments.

Moreover, you are kept fully informed in relation to new concepts, methods, practices, and directions in the field.

You discover that you are actually taking the examination all the time: you are preparing for the examination by "taking" an examination, not by reading extraneous and/or supererogatory textbooks.

In short, this PASSBOOK®, used directedly, should be an important factor in helping you to pass your test.

SENIOR BRIDGE AND TUNNEL MAINTAINER

DUTIES AND RESPONSIBILITIES
Under general direction, supervises and takes part in the maintenance and operation of the varied facilities and equipment of the bridge and tunnel authority; performs related work.

EXAMPLES OF TYPICAL TASKS
Supervises the work of assigned personnel in the maintenance of buildings, fixed and movable bridges, tunnels, and parts of the foregoing structures. Maintains and makes repairs to electrical wiring systems, power and control equipment, mechanical and structural devices which are normal to the facilities of the authority. Climbs bridge structures and main suspension cables and performs work on same. Supervises and takes part in the operation and maintenance of automotive and other mobile equipment, clearing and cleaning of buildings, bridges, approaches, tunnels and shops required for the continued operation of the authority's facilities.

TESTS
The written test may consist of questions on safety, supervision, painting, the maintenance and repair of automotive equipment, electrical installations, plumbing and heating installations, buildings, structures; and related areas.

HOW TO TAKE A TEST

I. YOU MUST PASS AN EXAMINATION

A. *WHAT EVERY CANDIDATE SHOULD KNOW*

Examination applicants often ask us for help in preparing for the written test. What can I study in advance? What kinds of questions will be asked? How will the test be given? How will the papers be graded?

As an applicant for a civil service examination, you may be wondering about some of these things. Our purpose here is to suggest effective methods of advance study and to describe civil service examinations.

Your chances for success on this examination can be increased if you know how to prepare. Those "pre-examination jitters" can be reduced if you know what to expect. You can even experience an adventure in good citizenship if you know why civil service exams are given.

B. *WHY ARE CIVIL SERVICE EXAMINATIONS GIVEN?*

Civil service examinations are important to you in two ways. As a citizen, you want public jobs filled by employees who know how to do their work. As a job seeker, you want a fair chance to compete for that job on an equal footing with other candidates. The best-known means of accomplishing this two-fold goal is the competitive examination.

Exams are widely publicized throughout the nation. They may be administered for jobs in federal, state, city, municipal, town or village governments or agencies.

Any citizen may apply, with some limitations, such as the age or residence of applicants. Your experience and education may be reviewed to see whether you meet the requirements for the particular examination. When these requirements exist, they are reasonable and applied consistently to all applicants. Thus, a competitive examination may cause you some uneasiness now, but it is your privilege and safeguard.

C. *HOW ARE CIVIL SERVICE EXAMS DEVELOPED?*

Examinations are carefully written by trained technicians who are specialists in the field known as "psychological measurement," in consultation with recognized authorities in the field of work that the test will cover. These experts recommend the subject matter areas or skills to be tested; only those knowledges or skills important to your success on the job are included. The most reliable books and source materials available are used as references. Together, the experts and technicians judge the difficulty level of the questions.

Test technicians know how to phrase questions so that the problem is clearly stated. Their ethics do not permit "trick" or "catch" questions. Questions may have been tried out on sample groups, or subjected to statistical analysis, to determine their usefulness.

Written tests are often used in combination with performance tests, ratings of training and experience, and oral interviews. All of these measures combine to form the best-known means of finding the right person for the right job.

II. HOW TO PASS THE WRITTEN TEST

A. NATURE OF THE EXAMINATION

To prepare intelligently for civil service examinations, you should know how they differ from school examinations you have taken. In school you were assigned certain definite pages to read or subjects to cover. The examination questions were quite detailed and usually emphasized memory. Civil service exams, on the other hand, try to discover your present ability to perform the duties of a position, plus your potentiality to learn these duties. In other words, a civil service exam attempts to predict how successful you will be. Questions cover such a broad area that they cannot be as minute and detailed as school exam questions.

In the public service similar kinds of work, or positions, are grouped together in one "class." This process is known as *position-classification*. All the positions in a class are paid according to the salary range for that class. One class title covers all of these positions, and they are all tested by the same examination.

B. FOUR BASIC STEPS

1) Study the announcement

How, then, can you know what subjects to study? Our best answer is: "Learn as much as possible about the class of positions for which you've applied." The exam will test the knowledge, skills and abilities needed to do the work.

Your most valuable source of information about the position you want is the official exam announcement. This announcement lists the training and experience qualifications. Check these standards and apply only if you come reasonably close to meeting them.

The brief description of the position in the examination announcement offers some clues to the subjects which will be tested. Think about the job itself. Review the duties in your mind. Can you perform them, or are there some in which you are rusty? Fill in the blank spots in your preparation.

Many jurisdictions preview the written test in the exam announcement by including a section called "Knowledge and Abilities Required," "Scope of the Examination," or some similar heading. Here you will find out specifically what fields will be tested.

2) Review your own background

Once you learn in general what the position is all about, and what you need to know to do the work, ask yourself which subjects you already know fairly well and which need improvement. You may wonder whether to concentrate on improving your strong areas or on building some background in your fields of weakness. When the announcement has specified "some knowledge" or "considerable knowledge," or has used adjectives like "beginning principles of…" or "advanced … methods," you can get a clue as to the number and difficulty of questions to be asked in any given field. More questions, and hence broader coverage, would be included for those subjects which are more important in the work. Now weigh your strengths and weaknesses against the job requirements and prepare accordingly.

3) Determine the level of the position

Another way to tell how intensively you should prepare is to understand the level of the job for which you are applying. Is it the entering level? In other words, is this the position in which beginners in a field of work are hired? Or is it an intermediate or advanced level? Sometimes this is indicated by such words as "Junior" or "Senior" in the class title. Other jurisdictions use Roman numerals to designate the level – Clerk I, Clerk II, for example. The word "Supervisor" sometimes appears in the title. If the level is not indicated by the title, check the description of duties. Will you be working under very close supervision, or will you have responsibility for independent decisions in this work?

4) Choose appropriate study materials

Now that you know the subjects to be examined and the relative amount of each subject to be covered, you can choose suitable study materials. For beginning level jobs, or even advanced ones, if you have a pronounced weakness in some aspect of your training, read a modern, standard textbook in that field. Be sure it is up to date and has general coverage. Such books are normally available at your library, and the librarian will be glad to help you locate one. For entry-level positions, questions of appropriate difficulty are chosen – neither highly advanced questions, nor those too simple. Such questions require careful thought but not advanced training.

If the position for which you are applying is technical or advanced, you will read more advanced, specialized material. If you are already familiar with the basic principles of your field, elementary textbooks would waste your time. Concentrate on advanced textbooks and technical periodicals. Think through the concepts and review difficult problems in your field.

These are all general sources. You can get more ideas on your own initiative, following these leads. For example, training manuals and publications of the government agency which employs workers in your field can be useful, particularly for technical and professional positions. A letter or visit to the government department involved may result in more specific study suggestions, and certainly will provide you with a more definite idea of the exact nature of the position you are seeking.

III. KINDS OF TESTS

Tests are used for purposes other than measuring knowledge and ability to perform specified duties. For some positions, it is equally important to test ability to make adjustments to new situations or to profit from training. In others, basic mental abilities not dependent on information are essential. Questions which test these things may not appear as pertinent to the duties of the position as those which test for knowledge and information. Yet they are often highly important parts of a fair examination. For very general questions, it is almost impossible to help you direct your study efforts. What we can do is to point out some of the more common of these general abilities needed in public service positions and describe some typical questions.

1) General information

Broad, general information has been found useful for predicting job success in some kinds of work. This is tested in a variety of ways, from vocabulary lists to questions about current events. Basic background in some field of work, such as sociology or economics, may be sampled in a group of questions. Often these are principles which have become familiar to most persons through exposure rather than through formal training. It is difficult to advise you how to study for these questions; being alert to the world around you is our best suggestion.

2) Verbal ability

An example of an ability needed in many positions is verbal or language ability. Verbal ability is, in brief, the ability to use and understand words. Vocabulary and grammar tests are typical measures of this ability. Reading comprehension or paragraph interpretation questions are common in many kinds of civil service tests. You are given a paragraph of written material and asked to find its central meaning.

3) **Numerical ability**

Number skills can be tested by the familiar arithmetic problem, by checking paired lists of numbers to see which are alike and which are different, or by interpreting charts and graphs. In the latter test, a graph may be printed in the test booklet which you are asked to use as the basis for answering questions.

4) **Observation**

A popular test for law-enforcement positions is the observation test. A picture is shown to you for several minutes, then taken away. Questions about the picture test your ability to observe both details and larger elements.

5) **Following directions**

In many positions in the public service, the employee must be able to carry out written instructions dependably and accurately. You may be given a chart with several columns, each column listing a variety of information. The questions require you to carry out directions involving the information given in the chart.

6) **Skills and aptitudes**

Performance tests effectively measure some manual skills and aptitudes. When the skill is one in which you are trained, such as typing or shorthand, you can practice. These tests are often very much like those given in business school or high school courses. For many of the other skills and aptitudes, however, no short-time preparation can be made. Skills and abilities natural to you or that you have developed throughout your lifetime are being tested.

Many of the general questions just described provide all the data needed to answer the questions and ask you to use your reasoning ability to find the answers. Your best preparation for these tests, as well as for tests of facts and ideas, is to be at your physical and mental best. You, no doubt, have your own methods of getting into an exam-taking mood and keeping "in shape." The next section lists some ideas on this subject.

IV. KINDS OF QUESTIONS

Only rarely is the "essay" question, which you answer in narrative form, used in civil service tests. Civil service tests are usually of the short-answer type. Full instructions for answering these questions will be given to you at the examination. But in case this is your first experience with short-answer questions and separate answer sheets, here is what you need to know:

1) Multiple-choice Questions

Most popular of the short-answer questions is the "multiple choice" or "best answer" question. It can be used, for example, to test for factual knowledge, ability to solve problems or judgment in meeting situations found at work.

A multiple-choice question is normally one of three types—

- It can begin with an incomplete statement followed by several possible endings. You are to find the one ending which *best* completes the statement, although some of the others may not be entirely wrong.
- It can also be a complete statement in the form of a question which is answered by choosing one of the statements listed.

- It can be in the form of a problem – again you select the best answer.

Here is an example of a multiple-choice question with a discussion which should give you some clues as to the method for choosing the right answer:

When an employee has a complaint about his assignment, the action which will *best* help him overcome his difficulty is to
    A. discuss his difficulty with his coworkers
    B. take the problem to the head of the organization
    C. take the problem to the person who gave him the assignment
    D. say nothing to anyone about his complaint

In answering this question, you should study each of the choices to find which is best. Consider choice "A" – Certainly an employee may discuss his complaint with fellow employees, but no change or improvement can result, and the complaint remains unresolved. Choice "B" is a poor choice since the head of the organization probably does not know what assignment you have been given, and taking your problem to him is known as "going over the head" of the supervisor. The supervisor, or person who made the assignment, is the person who can clarify it or correct any injustice. Choice "C" is, therefore, correct. To say nothing, as in choice "D," is unwise. Supervisors have and interest in knowing the problems employees are facing, and the employee is seeking a solution to his problem.

2) True/False Questions

The "true/false" or "right/wrong" form of question is sometimes used. Here a complete statement is given. Your job is to decide whether the statement is right or wrong.

SAMPLE: A roaming cell-phone call to a nearby city costs less than a non-roaming call to a distant city.

This statement is wrong, or false, since roaming calls are more expensive.

This is not a complete list of all possible question forms, although most of the others are variations of these common types. You will always get complete directions for answering questions. Be sure you understand *how* to mark your answers – ask questions until you do.

V. RECORDING YOUR ANSWERS

Computer terminals are used more and more today for many different kinds of exams.
For an examination with very few applicants, you may be told to record your answers in the test booklet itself. Separate answer sheets are much more common. If this separate answer sheet is to be scored by machine – and this is often the case – it is highly important that you mark your answers correctly in order to get credit.
An electronic scoring machine is often used in civil service offices because of the speed with which papers can be scored. Machine-scored answer sheets must be marked with a pencil, which will be given to you. This pencil has a high graphite content which responds to the electronic scoring machine. As a matter of fact, stray dots may register as answers, so do not let your pencil rest on the answer sheet while you are pondering the correct answer. Also, if your pencil lead breaks or is otherwise defective, ask for another.

Since the answer sheet will be dropped in a slot in the scoring machine, be careful not to bend the corners or get the paper crumpled.

The answer sheet normally has five vertical columns of numbers, with 30 numbers to a column. These numbers correspond to the question numbers in your test booklet. After each number, going across the page are four or five pairs of dotted lines. These short dotted lines have small letters or numbers above them. The first two pairs may also have a "T" or "F" above the letters. This indicates that the first two pairs only are to be used if the questions are of the true-false type. If the questions are multiple choice, disregard the "T" and "F" and pay attention only to the small letters or numbers.

Answer your questions in the manner of the sample that follows:

32. The largest city in the United States is
    A. Washington, D.C.
    B. New York City
    C. Chicago
    D. Detroit
    E. San Francisco

1) Choose the answer you think is best. (New York City is the largest, so "B" is correct.)
2) Find the row of dotted lines numbered the same as the question you are answering. (Find row number 32)
3) Find the pair of dotted lines corresponding to the answer. (Find the pair of lines under the mark "B.")
4) Make a solid black mark between the dotted lines.

VI. BEFORE THE TEST

Common sense will help you find procedures to follow to get ready for an examination. Too many of us, however, overlook these sensible measures. Indeed, nervousness and fatigue have been found to be the most serious reasons why applicants fail to do their best on civil service tests. Here is a list of reminders:

- Begin your preparation early – Don't wait until the last minute to go scurrying around for books and materials or to find out what the position is all about.
- Prepare continuously – An hour a night for a week is better than an all-night cram session. This has been definitely established. What is more, a night a week for a month will return better dividends than crowding your study into a shorter period of time.
- Locate the place of the exam – You have been sent a notice telling you when and where to report for the examination. If the location is in a different town or otherwise unfamiliar to you, it would be well to inquire the best route and learn something about the building.
- Relax the night before the test – Allow your mind to rest. Do not study at all that night. Plan some mild recreation or diversion; then go to bed early and get a good night's sleep.
- Get up early enough to make a leisurely trip to the place for the test – This way unforeseen events, traffic snarls, unfamiliar buildings, etc. will not upset you.
- Dress comfortably – A written test is not a fashion show. You will be known by number and not by name, so wear something comfortable.

- Leave excess paraphernalia at home – Shopping bags and odd bundles will get in your way. You need bring only the items mentioned in the official notice you received; usually everything you need is provided. Do not bring reference books to the exam. They will only confuse those last minutes and be taken away from you when in the test room.
- Arrive somewhat ahead of time – If because of transportation schedules you must get there very early, bring a newspaper or magazine to take your mind off yourself while waiting.
- Locate the examination room – When you have found the proper room, you will be directed to the seat or part of the room where you will sit. Sometimes you are given a sheet of instructions to read while you are waiting. Do not fill out any forms until you are told to do so; just read them and be prepared.
- Relax and prepare to listen to the instructions
- If you have any physical problem that may keep you from doing your best, be sure to tell the test administrator. If you are sick or in poor health, you really cannot do your best on the exam. You can come back and take the test some other time.

VII. AT THE TEST

The day of the test is here and you have the test booklet in your hand. The temptation to get going is very strong. Caution! There is more to success than knowing the right answers. You must know how to identify your papers and understand variations in the type of short-answer question used in this particular examination. Follow these suggestions for maximum results from your efforts:

1) Cooperate with the monitor

The test administrator has a duty to create a situation in which you can be as much at ease as possible. He will give instructions, tell you when to begin, check to see that you are marking your answer sheet correctly, and so on. He is not there to guard you, although he will see that your competitors do not take unfair advantage. He wants to help you do your best.

2) Listen to all instructions

Don't jump the gun! Wait until you understand all directions. In most civil service tests you get more time than you need to answer the questions. So don't be in a hurry. Read each word of instructions until you clearly understand the meaning. Study the examples, listen to all announcements and follow directions. Ask questions if you do not understand what to do.

3) Identify your papers

Civil service exams are usually identified by number only. You will be assigned a number; you must not put your name on your test papers. Be sure to copy your number correctly. Since more than one exam may be given, copy your exact examination title.

4) Plan your time

Unless you are told that a test is a "speed" or "rate of work" test, speed itself is usually not important. Time enough to answer all the questions will be provided, but this does not mean that you have all day. An overall time limit has been set. Divide the total time (in minutes) by the number of questions to determine the approximate time you have for each question.

5) Do not linger over difficult questions

If you come across a difficult question, mark it with a paper clip (useful to have along) and come back to it when you have been through the booklet. One caution if you do this – be sure to skip a number on your answer sheet as well. Check often to be sure that you have not lost your place and that you are marking in the row numbered the same as the question you are answering.

6) Read the questions

Be sure you know what the question asks! Many capable people are unsuccessful because they failed to *read* the questions correctly.

7) Answer all questions

Unless you have been instructed that a penalty will be deducted for incorrect answers, it is better to guess than to omit a question.

8) Speed tests

It is often better NOT to guess on speed tests. It has been found that on timed tests people are tempted to spend the last few seconds before time is called in marking answers at random – without even reading them – in the hope of picking up a few extra points. To discourage this practice, the instructions may warn you that your score will be "corrected" for guessing. That is, a penalty will be applied. The incorrect answers will be deducted from the correct ones, or some other penalty formula will be used.

9) Review your answers

If you finish before time is called, go back to the questions you guessed or omitted to give them further thought. Review other answers if you have time.

10) Return your test materials

If you are ready to leave before others have finished or time is called, take ALL your materials to the monitor and leave quietly. Never take any test material with you. The monitor can discover whose papers are not complete, and taking a test booklet may be grounds for disqualification.

VIII. EXAMINATION TECHNIQUES

1) Read the general instructions carefully. These are usually printed on the first page of the exam booklet. As a rule, these instructions refer to the timing of the examination; the fact that you should not start work until the signal and must stop work at a signal, etc. If there are any *special* instructions, such as a choice of questions to be answered, make sure that you note this instruction carefully.

2) When you are ready to start work on the examination, that is as soon as the signal has been given, read the instructions to each question booklet, underline any key words or phrases, such as *least, best, outline, describe* and the like. In this way you will tend to answer as requested rather than discover on reviewing your paper that you *listed without describing*, that you selected the *worst* choice rather than the *best* choice, etc.

3) If the examination is of the objective or multiple-choice type – that is, each question will also give a series of possible answers: A, B, C or D, and you are called upon to select the best answer and write the letter next to that answer on your answer paper – it is advisable to start answering each question in turn. There may be anywhere from 50 to 100 such questions in the three or four hours allotted and you can see how much time would be taken if you read through all the questions before beginning to answer any. Furthermore, if you come across a question or group of questions which you know would be difficult to answer, it would undoubtedly affect your handling of all the other questions.

4) If the examination is of the essay type and contains but a few questions, it is a moot point as to whether you should read all the questions before starting to answer any one. Of course, if you are given a choice – say five out of seven and the like – then it is essential to read all the questions so you can eliminate the two that are most difficult. If, however, you are asked to answer all the questions, there may be danger in trying to answer the easiest one first because you may find that you will spend too much time on it. The best technique is to answer the first question, then proceed to the second, etc.

5) Time your answers. Before the exam begins, write down the time it started, then add the time allowed for the examination and write down the time it must be completed, then divide the time available somewhat as follows:
    - If 3-1/2 hours are allowed, that would be 210 minutes. If you have 80 objective-type questions, that would be an average of 2-1/2 minutes per question. Allow yourself no more than 2 minutes per question, or a total of 160 minutes, which will permit about 50 minutes to review.
    - If for the time allotment of 210 minutes there are 7 essay questions to answer, that would average about 30 minutes a question. Give yourself only 25 minutes per question so that you have about 35 minutes to review.

6) The most important instruction is to *read each question* and make sure you know what is wanted. The second most important instruction is to *time yourself properly* so that you answer every question. The third most important instruction is to *answer every question*. Guess if you have to but include something for each question. Remember that you will receive no credit for a blank and will probably receive some credit if you write something in answer to an essay question. If you guess a letter – say "B" for a multiple-choice question – you may have guessed right. If you leave a blank as an answer to a multiple-choice question, the examiners may respect your feelings but it will not add a point to your score. Some exams may penalize you for wrong answers, so in such cases *only*, you may not want to guess unless you have some basis for your answer.

7) Suggestions
    a. Objective-type questions
        1. Examine the question booklet for proper sequence of pages and questions
        2. Read all instructions carefully
        3. Skip any question which seems too difficult; return to it after all other questions have been answered
        4. Apportion your time properly; do not spend too much time on any single question or group of questions

5. Note and underline key words – *all, most, fewest, least, best, worst, same, opposite,* etc.
6. Pay particular attention to negatives
7. Note unusual option, e.g., unduly long, short, complex, different or similar in content to the body of the question
8. Observe the use of "hedging" words – *probably, may, most likely,* etc.
9. Make sure that your answer is put next to the same number as the question
10. Do not second-guess unless you have good reason to believe the second answer is definitely more correct
11. Cross out original answer if you decide another answer is more accurate; do not erase until you are ready to hand your paper in
12. Answer all questions; guess unless instructed otherwise
13. Leave time for review

   b. Essay questions
   1. Read each question carefully
   2. Determine exactly what is wanted. Underline key words or phrases.
   3. Decide on outline or paragraph answer
   4. Include many different points and elements unless asked to develop any one or two points or elements
   5. Show impartiality by giving pros and cons unless directed to select one side only
   6. Make and write down any assumptions you find necessary to answer the questions
   7. Watch your English, grammar, punctuation and choice of words
   8. Time your answers; don't crowd material

8) Answering the essay question

Most essay questions can be answered by framing the specific response around several key words or ideas. Here are a few such key words or ideas:

M's: manpower, materials, methods, money, management
P's: purpose, program, policy, plan, procedure, practice, problems, pitfalls, personnel, public relations

   a. Six basic steps in handling problems:
   1. Preliminary plan and background development
   2. Collect information, data and facts
   3. Analyze and interpret information, data and facts
   4. Analyze and develop solutions as well as make recommendations
   5. Prepare report and sell recommendations
   6. Install recommendations and follow up effectiveness

   b. Pitfalls to avoid
   1. *Taking things for granted* – A statement of the situation does not necessarily imply that each of the elements is necessarily true; for example, a complaint may be invalid and biased so that all that can be taken for granted is that a complaint has been registered

2. *Considering only one side of a situation* – Wherever possible, indicate several alternatives and then point out the reasons you selected the best one
3. *Failing to indicate follow up* – Whenever your answer indicates action on your part, make certain that you will take proper follow-up action to see how successful your recommendations, procedures or actions turn out to be
4. *Taking too long in answering any single question* – Remember to time your answers properly

IX. AFTER THE TEST

Scoring procedures differ in detail among civil service jurisdictions although the general principles are the same. Whether the papers are hand-scored or graded by machine we have described, they are nearly always graded by number. That is, the person who marks the paper knows only the number – never the name – of the applicant. Not until all the papers have been graded will they be matched with names. If other tests, such as training and experience or oral interview ratings have been given, scores will be combined. Different parts of the examination usually have different weights. For example, the written test might count 60 percent of the final grade, and a rating of training and experience 40 percent. In many jurisdictions, veterans will have a certain number of points added to their grades.

After the final grade has been determined, the names are placed in grade order and an eligible list is established. There are various methods for resolving ties between those who get the same final grade – probably the most common is to place first the name of the person whose application was received first. Job offers are made from the eligible list in the order the names appear on it. You will be notified of your grade and your rank as soon as all these computations have been made. This will be done as rapidly as possible.

People who are found to meet the requirements in the announcement are called "eligibles." Their names are put on a list of eligible candidates. An eligible's chances of getting a job depend on how high he stands on this list and how fast agencies are filling jobs from the list.

When a job is to be filled from a list of eligibles, the agency asks for the names of people on the list of eligibles for that job. When the civil service commission receives this request, it sends to the agency the names of the three people highest on this list. Or, if the job to be filled has specialized requirements, the office sends the agency the names of the top three persons who meet these requirements from the general list.

The appointing officer makes a choice from among the three people whose names were sent to him. If the selected person accepts the appointment, the names of the others are put back on the list to be considered for future openings.

That is the rule in hiring from all kinds of eligible lists, whether they are for typist, carpenter, chemist, or something else. For every vacancy, the appointing officer has his choice of any one of the top three eligibles on the list. This explains why the person whose name is on top of the list sometimes does not get an appointment when some of the persons lower on the list do. If the appointing officer chooses the second or third eligible, the No. 1 eligible does not get a job at once, but stays on the list until he is appointed or the list is terminated.

X. HOW TO PASS THE INTERVIEW TEST

The examination for which you applied requires an oral interview test. You have already taken the written test and you are now being called for the interview test – the final part of the formal examination.

You may think that it is not possible to prepare for an interview test and that there are no procedures to follow during an interview. Our purpose is to point out some things you can do in advance that will help you and some good rules to follow and pitfalls to avoid while you are being interviewed.

What is an interview supposed to test?

The written examination is designed to test the technical knowledge and competence of the candidate; the oral is designed to evaluate intangible qualities, not readily measured otherwise, and to establish a list showing the relative fitness of each candidate – as measured against his competitors – for the position sought. Scoring is not on the basis of "right" and "wrong," but on a sliding scale of values ranging from "not passable" to "outstanding." As a matter of fact, it is possible to achieve a relatively low score without a single "incorrect" answer because of evident weakness in the qualities being measured.

Occasionally, an examination may consist entirely of an oral test – either an individual or a group oral. In such cases, information is sought concerning the technical knowledges and abilities of the candidate, since there has been no written examination for this purpose. More commonly, however, an oral test is used to supplement a written examination.

Who conducts interviews?

The composition of oral boards varies among different jurisdictions. In nearly all, a representative of the personnel department serves as chairman. One of the members of the board may be a representative of the department in which the candidate would work. In some cases, "outside experts" are used, and, frequently, a businessman or some other representative of the general public is asked to serve. Labor and management or other special groups may be represented. The aim is to secure the services of experts in the appropriate field.

However the board is composed, it is a good idea (and not at all improper or unethical) to ascertain in advance of the interview who the members are and what groups they represent. When you are introduced to them, you will have some idea of their backgrounds and interests, and at least you will not stutter and stammer over their names.

What should be done before the interview?

While knowledge about the board members is useful and takes some of the surprise element out of the interview, there is other preparation which is more substantive. It *is* possible to prepare for an oral interview – in several ways:

1) Keep a copy of your application and review it carefully before the interview

This may be the only document before the oral board, and the starting point of the interview. Know what education and experience you have listed there, and the sequence and dates of all of it. Sometimes the board will ask you to review the highlights of your experience for them; you should not have to hem and haw doing it.

2) Study the class specification and the examination announcement

Usually, the oral board has one or both of these to guide them. The qualities, characteristics or knowledges required by the position sought are stated in these documents. They offer valuable clues as to the nature of the oral interview. For example, if the job involves supervisory responsibilities, the announcement will usually indicate that knowledge of modern supervisory methods and the qualifications of the candidate as a supervisor will be tested. If so, you can expect such questions, frequently in the form of a hypothetical situation which you are expected to solve. NEVER go into an oral without knowledge of the duties and responsibilities of the job you seek.

3) Think through each qualification required

Try to visualize the kind of questions you would ask if you were a board member. How well could you answer them? Try especially to appraise your own knowledge and background in each area, *measured against the job sought*, and identify any areas in which you are weak. Be critical and realistic – do not flatter yourself.

4) Do some general reading in areas in which you feel you may be weak

For example, if the job involves supervision and your past experience has NOT, some general reading in supervisory methods and practices, particularly in the field of human relations, might be useful. Do NOT study agency procedures or detailed manuals. The oral board will be testing your understanding and capacity, not your memory.

5) Get a good night's sleep and watch your general health and mental attitude

You will want a clear head at the interview. Take care of a cold or any other minor ailment, and of course, no hangovers.

What should be done on the day of the interview?

Now comes the day of the interview itself. Give yourself plenty of time to get there. Plan to arrive somewhat ahead of the scheduled time, particularly if your appointment is in the fore part of the day. If a previous candidate fails to appear, the board might be ready for you a bit early. By early afternoon an oral board is almost invariably behind schedule if there are many candidates, and you may have to wait. Take along a book or magazine to read, or your application to review, but leave any extraneous material in the waiting room when you go in for your interview. In any event, relax and compose yourself.

The matter of dress is important. The board is forming impressions about you – from your experience, your manners, your attitude, and your appearance. Give your personal appearance careful attention. Dress your best, but not your flashiest. Choose conservative, appropriate clothing, and be sure it is immaculate. This is a business interview, and your appearance should indicate that you regard it as such. Besides, being well groomed and properly dressed will help boost your confidence.

Sooner or later, someone will call your name and escort you into the interview room. *This is it.* From here on you are on your own. It is too late for any more preparation. But remember, you asked for this opportunity to prove your fitness, and you are here because your request was granted.

What happens when you go in?

The usual sequence of events will be as follows: The clerk (who is often the board stenographer) will introduce you to the chairman of the oral board, who will introduce you to the other members of the board. Acknowledge the introductions before you sit down. Do not be surprised if you find a microphone facing you or a stenotypist sitting by. Oral interviews are usually recorded in the event of an appeal or other review.

Usually the chairman of the board will open the interview by reviewing the highlights of your education and work experience from your application – primarily for the benefit of the other members of the board, as well as to get the material into the record. Do not interrupt or comment unless there is an error or significant misinterpretation; if that is the case, do not hesitate. But do not quibble about insignificant matters. Also, he will usually ask you some question about your education, experience or your present job – partly to get you to start talking and to establish the interviewing "rapport." He may start the actual questioning, or turn it over to one of the other members. Frequently, each member undertakes the questioning on a particular area, one in which he is perhaps most competent, so you can expect each member to participate in the examination. Because time is limited, you may also expect some rather abrupt switches in the direction the questioning takes, so do not be upset by it. Normally, a board member will not pursue a single line of questioning unless he discovers a particular strength or weakness.

After each member has participated, the chairman will usually ask whether any member has any further questions, then will ask you if you have anything you wish to add. Unless you are expecting this question, it may floor you. Worse, it may start you off on an extended, extemporaneous speech. The board is not usually seeking more information. The question is principally to offer you a last opportunity to present further qualifications or to indicate that you have nothing to add. So, if you feel that a significant qualification or characteristic has been overlooked, it is proper to point it out in a sentence or so. Do not compliment the board on the thoroughness of their examination – they have been sketchy, and you know it. If you wish, merely say, "No thank you, I have nothing further to add." This is a point where you can "talk yourself out" of a good impression or fail to present an important bit of information. Remember, *you close the interview yourself*.

The chairman will then say, "That is all, Mr. _____, thank you." Do not be startled; the interview is over, and quicker than you think. Thank him, gather your belongings and take your leave. Save your sigh of relief for the other side of the door.

How to put your best foot forward

Throughout this entire process, you may feel that the board individually and collectively is trying to pierce your defenses, seek out your hidden weaknesses and embarrass and confuse you. Actually, this is not true. They are obliged to make an appraisal of your qualifications for the job you are seeking, and they want to see you in your best light. Remember, they must interview all candidates and a non-cooperative candidate may become a failure in spite of their best efforts to bring out his qualifications. Here are 15 suggestions that will help you:

1) Be natural – Keep your attitude confident, not cocky

If you are not confident that you can do the job, do not expect the board to be. Do not apologize for your weaknesses, try to bring out your strong points. The board is interested in a positive, not negative, presentation. Cockiness will antagonize any board member and make him wonder if you are covering up a weakness by a false show of strength.

2) Get comfortable, but don't lounge or sprawl

Sit erectly but not stiffly. A careless posture may lead the board to conclude that you are careless in other things, or at least that you are not impressed by the importance of the occasion. Either conclusion is natural, even if incorrect. Do not fuss with your clothing, a pencil or an ashtray. Your hands may occasionally be useful to emphasize a point; do not let them become a point of distraction.

3) Do not wisecrack or make small talk

This is a serious situation, and your attitude should show that you consider it as such. Further, the time of the board is limited – they do not want to waste it, and neither should you.

4) Do not exaggerate your experience or abilities

In the first place, from information in the application or other interviews and sources, the board may know more about you than you think. Secondly, you probably will not get away with it. An experienced board is rather adept at spotting such a situation, so do not take the chance.

5) If you know a board member, do not make a point of it, yet do not hide it

Certainly you are not fooling him, and probably not the other members of the board. Do not try to take advantage of your acquaintanceship – it will probably do you little good.

6) Do not dominate the interview

Let the board do that. They will give you the clues – do not assume that you have to do all the talking. Realize that the board has a number of questions to ask you, and do not try to take up all the interview time by showing off your extensive knowledge of the answer to the first one.

7) Be attentive

You only have 20 minutes or so, and you should keep your attention at its sharpest throughout. When a member is addressing a problem or question to you, give him your undivided attention. Address your reply principally to him, but do not exclude the other board members.

8) Do not interrupt

A board member may be stating a problem for you to analyze. He will ask you a question when the time comes. Let him state the problem, and wait for the question.

9) Make sure you understand the question

Do not try to answer until you are sure what the question is. If it is not clear, restate it in your own words or ask the board member to clarify it for you. However, do not haggle about minor elements.

10) Reply promptly but not hastily

A common entry on oral board rating sheets is "candidate responded readily," or "candidate hesitated in replies." Respond as promptly and quickly as you can, but do not jump to a hasty, ill-considered answer.

11) Do not be peremptory in your answers

A brief answer is proper – but do not fire your answer back. That is a losing game from your point of view. The board member can probably ask questions much faster than you can answer them.

12) Do not try to create the answer you think the board member wants

He is interested in what kind of mind you have and how it works – not in playing games. Furthermore, he can usually spot this practice and will actually grade you down on it.

13) Do not switch sides in your reply merely to agree with a board member

Frequently, a member will take a contrary position merely to draw you out and to see if you are willing and able to defend your point of view. Do not start a debate, yet do not surrender a good position. If a position is worth taking, it is worth defending.

14) Do not be afraid to admit an error in judgment if you are shown to be wrong

The board knows that you are forced to reply without any opportunity for careful consideration. Your answer may be demonstrably wrong. If so, admit it and get on with the interview.

15) Do not dwell at length on your present job

The opening question may relate to your present assignment. Answer the question but do not go into an extended discussion. You are being examined for a *new* job, not your present one. As a matter of fact, try to phrase ALL your answers in terms of the job for which you are being examined.

Basis of Rating

Probably you will forget most of these "do's" and "don'ts" when you walk into the oral interview room. Even remembering them all will not ensure you a passing grade. Perhaps you did not have the qualifications in the first place. But remembering them will help you to put your best foot forward, without treading on the toes of the board members.

Rumor and popular opinion to the contrary notwithstanding, an oral board wants you to make the best appearance possible. They know you are under pressure – but they also want to see how you respond to it as a guide to what your reaction would be under the pressures of the job you seek. They will be influenced by the degree of poise you display, the personal traits you show and the manner in which you respond.

ABOUT THIS BOOK

This book contains tests divided into Examination Sections. Go through each test, answering every question in the margin. We have also attached a sample answer sheet at the back of the book that can be removed and used. At the end of each test look at the answer key and check your answers. On the ones you got wrong, look at the right answer choice and learn. Do not fill in the answers first. Do not memorize the questions and answers, but understand the answer and principles involved. On your test, the questions will likely be different from the samples. Questions are changed and new ones added. If you understand these past questions you should have success with any changes that arise. Tests may consist of several types of questions. We have additional books on each subject should more study be advisable or necessary for you. Finally, the more you study, the better prepared you will be. This book is intended to be the last thing you study before you walk into the examination room. Prior study of relevant texts is also recommended. NLC publishes some of these in our Fundamental Series. Knowledge and good sense are important factors in passing your exam. Good luck also helps. So now study this Passbook, absorb the material contained within and take that knowledge into the examination. Then do your best to pass that exam.

EXAMINATION SECTION

EXAMINATION SECTION
TEST 1

DIRECTIONS: Each question or incomplete statement is followed by several suggested answers or completions. Select the one that BEST answers the question or completes the statement. *PRINT THE LETTER OF THE CORRECT ANSWER IN THE SPACE AT THE RIGHT.*

1. A bit is held in a hand drill by means of a(n)

    A. arbor B. chuck C. collet D. clamp

2. The type of screw that MOST often requires a countersunk hole is a _____ head.

    A. flat B. round C. fillister D. hexagon

3. Instead of using the ordinary 1 piece screwdriver, a screwdriver bit is MOST often used with a brace because of the

    A. increased length of the brace
    B. different types of bits available
    C. increased leverage of the brace
    D. ability to work in tight corners

4. A thread gage is usually used to measure the

    A. thickness of a thread
    B. diameter of a thread
    C. number of threads per inch
    D. height of a thread

5. The wheel of a glass cutter is BEST lubricated with

    A. kerosene
    B. linseed oil
    C. varnolene
    D. diesel oil

6. A nail set is a

    A. group of nails of the same size and type
    B. group of nails of different sizes but the same type
    C. tool used to extract nails
    D. tool used to drive nails below the surface of wood

7. To test for leaks in a gas line, it is BEST to use

    A. a match
    B. soapy water
    C. a colored dye
    D. ammonia

8. Routing is the process of cutting a

    A. strip out of sheet metal
    B. groove in wood
    C. chamfer on a shaft
    D. core out of concrete

9. A hacksaw frame has a wing nut mainly to

    A. make it easier to replace blades
    B. increase the strength of the frame
    C. prevent vibration of the blade
    D. adjust the length of the frame

10. A mitre box is usually used with a _____ saw. 10.____
    A. hack   B. crosscut   C. rip   D. back

11. A continuous flexible saw blade is MOST often used on a _____ saw. 11.____
    A. radial   B. band   C. swing   D. table

12. A pipe reamer is used to 12.____
    A. clean out a length of pipe
    B. thread pipe
    C. remove burrs from the ends of pipe
    D. seal pipe joints

13. To lay out a straight cut on a piece of wood at the same angle as the cut on a second piece of wood, the PROPER tool to use is a 13.____
    A. bevel   B. cope   C. butt gauge   D. clevis

14. Before drilling a hole in a piece of metal, an indentation should be made with a _____ punch. 14.____
    A. pin   B. taper   C. center   D. drift

15. Curved cuts in wood are BEST made with a _____ saw. 15.____
    A. jig   B. veneer   C. radial   D. swing

16. A face plate is generally used to 16.____
    A. hold material while working with it on a lathe
    B. smooth out irregularities in a metal plate
    C. protect the finish on a metal plate
    D. locate centers of holes to be drilled on a drill press

17. A die would be used to 17.____
    A. gage the groove in a splined shaft
    B. cut a thread on a metal rod
    C. hold a piece to be machined on a milling machine
    D. control the depth of a hole to be drilled in a piece of metal

18. Before using a ladle to scoop up molten solder, you should make sure that the ladle is dry. 18.____
    This is done to prevent
    A. the solder from sticking to the ladle
    B. impurities from getting into the solder
    C. injuries due to splashing solder
    D. cooling of the solder

19. To PROPERLY adjust the gap on a spark plug, you should use a(n)   19._____

    A. inside caliper   B. center gauge
    C. wire type feeler gauge   D. micrometer

20. The length of the MOST common type of folding wood rule is _____ feet.   20._____

    A. 4   B. 5   C. 6   D. 7

21. A four-foot mason's level is usually used to determine whether the top of a wall is level and whether it is   21._____

    A. square   B. plumb   C. rigid   D. in line

22. To match a tongue in a board, the matching board MUST have a   22._____

    A. rabbet   B. chamfer   C. bead   D. groove

23. When driving screws in close quarters, the BEST type of screwdriver to use is a(n)   23._____

    A. Phillips   B. offset   C. butt   D. angled

24. The term 12-24 refers to a _____ screw.   24._____

    A. wood   B. lag
    C. sheet metal   D. machine

25. To measure the length of a curved line on a drawing or plan, the PROPER tool to use in addition to a ruler is(are)   25._____

    A. dividers   B. calipers
    C. surface gage   D. radius gage

26. For the standard machine screw, the diameter of a tap drill is generally   26._____

    A. *equal* to the diameter of the shaft of the screw at the base of the threads (the root diameter)
    B. *larger* than the root diameter, but smaller than the diameter of the screw
    C. *equal* to the diameter of the screw
    D. *larger* than the diameter of the screw

27. In order to drill a 1" hole accurately with a drill press, you should   27._____

    A. drill at high speeds
    B. use very little pressure on the drill
    C. drill partway down, release pressure on the drill, and then continue drilling
    D. drill a pilot hole first

28. Before taking apart an electric motor to repair, punch marks are sometimes placed on the casing near each other.   28._____
    The MOST probable reason for doing this is to

    A. make sure the parts lock together on reassembly
    B. properly line up the parts that are next to each other
    C. keep track of the number of parts in the assembly
    D. identify all the parts as coming from the one motor

29. To locate a point on a floor directly under a point on the ceiling, the PROPER tool to use is a

    A. square
    B. line level
    C. height gage
    D. plumb bob

Question 30.

DIRECTIONS: Question 30 is based on the diagram appearing below.

30. In the above diagram, the full P required to lift the weight a distance of four feet is MOST NEARLY _____ lbs.

    A. 50   B. 67   C. 75   D. 100

31. The EASIEST tool to use to determine whether the edge of a board is at right angles to the face of the board is a

    A. rafter square
    B. try square
    C. protractor
    D. marking gage

32. *Whetting* refers to

    A. tempering of tools by dipping them in water
    B. annealing of tools by heating and slow cooling
    C. brazing of carbide tips on tools
    D. sharpening of tools

33. The MOST difficult part of a plank to plane is the

    A. face   B. side   C. end   D. back

34. To prevent wood from splitting when drilling with an auger, it is BEST to

    A. use even pressure on the bit
    B. drill at a slow speed
    C. hold the wood tightly in a vise
    D. back up the wood with a piece of scrap wood

35. The term *dressing a grinding wheel* refers to 35._____

    A. setting up the wheel on the arbor
    B. restoring the sharpness of a wheel face that has become clogged
    C. placing flanges against the sides of the wheel
    D. bringing the wheel up to speed before using it

36. Heads of rivets are BEST cut off with a 36._____

    A. hacksaw   B. cold chisel
    C. fly cutter   D. reamer

37. A *V-block* is especially useful to 37._____

    A. prevent damage to work held in a vise
    B. hold round stock while a hole is being drilled into it
    C. prevent rolling of round stock stored on the ground
    D. shim up the end of a machine so that it is level

38. A full set of taps for a given size usually consists of a _____ tap. 38._____

    A. taper and bottoming
    B. taper and plug
    C. plug and bottoming
    D. taper, plug, and bottoming

39. Round thread cutting dies are usually held in stock by means of 39._____

    A. wing nuts   B. clamps   C. set screws   D. bolts

40. The one of the following diagrams that shows the plan view and the elevation of a counterbored hole is 40._____

A.

B.

C.

D.

41. With regard to pipe, *I.D.* usually means 41._____

    A. inside diameter   B. inside dressed
    C. invert diameter   D. installation date

42. A compression fitting is MOST often used to

   A. lubricate a wheel
   B. join two pieces of tubing
   C. reduce the diameter of a hole
   D. press fit a gear to a shaft

43. The shape of a mill file is basically

   A. flat   B. half round   C. triangular   D. square

44. Of the following, the ratio of tin to lead that will produce the solder with the LOWEST melting point is

   A. 30-70   B. 40-60   C. 50-50   D. 60-40

45. A safe edge on a file is one that

   A. is smooth and can not cut
   B. has a finer cut than the face of the file
   C. is rounded to prevent scratches
   D. has a coarser cut than the face of the file

46. The MOST frequent use of a file card is to _____ files.

   A. sort out   B. clean
   C. prevent damage to D. prevent clogging of

47. The BEST way of determining whether a grinding wheel has an internal crack is to

   A. run the wheel at high speed, stop it, and examine the wheel
   B. spray lubricating oil on the sides of the wheel and check the amount of absorption of the oil
   C. hit the wheel with a rubber hammer and listen to the sound
   D. drop the wheel sharply on a table and then check the wheel

48. If a grinding wheel has worn to a smaller diameter, the BEST practice to follow is to

   A. discard the wheel
   B. continue using the wheel as before
   C. use the wheel, but at a faster speed
   D. use the wheel, but at a slower speed

49. With respect to the ordinary awl,

   A. only the tip is hardened
   B. the entire blade is hardened
   C. the tip is tempered, and the rest of the blade is hardened
   D. the entire blade is tempered

50. To prevent overheating of drills, it is BEST to use _____ oil.

   A. cutting   B. lubricating
   C. penetrating   D. heating

KEY (CORRECT ANSWERS)

1. B	11. B	21. B	31. B	41. A
2. A	12. C	22. D	32. D	42. B
3. C	13. A	23. B	33. C	43. A
4. C	14. C	24. D	34. D	44. D
5. A	15. A	25. A	35. B	45. A
6. D	16. A	26. B	36. B	46. B
7. B	17. B	27. D	37. B	47. C
8. B	18. C	28. B	38. D	48. C
9. A	19. C	29. D	39. C	49. A
10. D	20. C	30. D	40. A	50. A

TEST 2

DIRECTIONS: Each question or incomplete statement is followed by several suggested answers or completions. Select the one that BEST answers the question or completes the statement. *PRINT THE LETTER OF THE CORRECT ANSWER IN THE SPACE AT THE RIGHT.*

1. Crocus cloth is commonly used to

   A. protect finely machined surfaces from damage while the machines are being repaired
   B. remove rust from steel
   C. protect floors and furniture while painting walls
   D. wipe up oil and grease that has spilled

   1._____

2. Before using a new paint brush, the FIRST operation should be to

   A. remove loose bristles
   B. soak the brush in linseed oil
   C. hang the brush up overnight
   D. clean the brush with turpentine

   2._____

3. When sharpening a hand saw, the FIRST operation is to

   A. file the teeth down to the same height
   B. shape the teeth to the proper profile
   C. bend the teeth over to provide clearance when sawing
   D. clean the gullies with a file

   3._____

4. To prevent solder from dripping when soldering a vertical seam, it is BEST to

   A. hold a waxed rag under the soldering iron
   B. use the soldering iron in a horizontal position
   C. tin the soldering iron on one side only
   D. solder the seam in the order from bottom to top

   4._____

5. If a round nut has two holes in the face, the PROPER type wrench to use to tighten this nut is a(n)

   A. Stillson   B. monkey   C. spanner   D. open end

   5._____

6. A box wrench is BEST used on

   A. pipe fittings   B. flare nuts
   C. hexagonal nuts   D. Allen screws

   6._____

7. To prevent damage to fine finishes on metal work that is to be held in a vise, you should

   A. clamp the work lightly
   B. use brass inserts on the vise
   C. wrap the work with cloth before inserting it in the vise
   D. substitute a smooth face plate for the serrated plate on the vise

   7._____

8. The MOST frequent use for a turnbuckle is to   8.____
   A. tighten a guy wire
   B. adjust shims on a machine
   C. bolt a bracket to a wall
   D. support electric cable from a ceiling

9. To form the head of a tinner's rivet, the PROPER tool to use is a rivet   9.____
   A. anvil   B. plate   C. set   D. brake

10. A socket speed handle MOST closely resembles a   10.____
    A. screwdriver   B. brace   C. spanner   D. spin grip

11. Tips of masonry drills are usually made of   11.____
    A. steel   B. carbide   C. corundum   D. monel

12. The BEST flux to use for soldering galvanized iron is   12.____
    A. resin   B. sal ammoniac
    C. borax   D. muriatic acid

13. The one of the following that is NOT a common type of oilstone is   13.____
    A. silicon carbide   B. aluminum oxide
    C. hard Arkansas   D. pumice

14. A method of joining metals using temperatures intermediate between soldering and welding is   14.____
    A. corbelling   B. brazing   C. annealing   D. lapping

15. When an unusually high degree of accuracy is required with woodwork, lines should be marked with a   15.____
    A. pencil ground to a chisel point
    B. pencil line over a crayon line
    C. sharp knife point
    D. scriber

16. The MOST important difference between pipe threads and V threads on bolts is that pipe threads are usually   16.____
    A. longer   B. sharper
    C. tapered   D. more evenly spaced

17. A street elbow differs from the ordinary elbow in that the street elbow has   17.____
    A. different diameter threads at each end
    B. male threads at one end and female threads at the other
    C. female threads at both ends
    D. male threads at both ends

18. Water hammer in a pipe line can MOST often be stopped by the installation of a(n)   18.____
    A. pressure reducing valve   B. expansion joint
    C. flexible coupling   D. air chamber

19. If water is leaking from the top part of a bibcock, the part that should be replaced is MOST likely the

    A. bibb washer
    B. packing
    C. seat
    D. bibb screw

20. When joining electric wires together in a fixture box, the BEST thing to use are wire

    A. connectors   B. couplings   C. clamps   D. bolts

21. If the name plate of a motor indicates that it is a split phase motor, it is LIKELY that this motor

    A. is a universal motor
    B. operates on DC only
    C. operates on AC only
    D. operates either on DC at full power or on AC at reduced power

22. To make driving of a screw into hard wood easier, it is BEST to lubricate the threads of the screw with

    A. varnoline
    B. penetrating oil
    C. beeswax
    D. cutting oil

23. Assume that a thermostatically controlled oil heater fails to operate. To determine whether it is the thermostat that is at fault, you should

    A. check the circuit breaker
    B. connect a wire across the terminals of the thermostat
    C. replace the contacts on the thermostat
    D. put an ammeter on the line

24. The function of the carburetor on a gasoline engine is to

    A. mix the air and gasoline properly
    B. filter the fuel
    C. filter the air to engine
    D. pump the gasoline into the cylinder

25. If a car owner complains that the battery in his car is constantly running dry, the item that should be checked FIRST is the

    A. fan belt
    B. generator
    C. voltage regulator
    D. relay

26. On MOST modern automobiles, foot brake pressure is transmitted to the brake drums by

    A. air pressure
    B. mechanical linkage
    C. hydraulic fluid
    D. electro-magnetic force

27. Assume that the engine of a car remains cold even though it is run for a period of time. The part that is MOST likely at fault is the

    A. heat by-pass valve
    B. thermostat
    C. heater control
    D. choke

28. To permit easy stripping of concrete forms, they should be   28._____
    A. dried   B. oiled   C. wet down   D. cleaned

29. To prevent honey combing in concrete, the concrete should be   29._____
    A. vibrated   B. cured
    C. heated in cold weather   D. protected from the rain

30. The MAIN reason for using wire mesh in connection with concrete work is to   30._____
    A. strain the impurities from the sand
    B. increase the strength of the concrete
    C. hold the forms together
    D. protect the concrete till it hardens

31. Segregation of concrete is MOST often caused by pouring concrete   31._____
    A. in cold weather
    B. from too great a height
    C. too rapidly
    D. into a form in which the concrete has already begun to harden

32. Headers in carpentry are MOST closely associated with   32._____
    A. trimmers   B. cantilevers
    C. posts   D. newels

33. Joists are very often supported by   33._____
    A. suspenders   B. base plates
    C. anchor bolts   D. bridal irons

34. At outside corners, the type of joint MOST frequently used on a baseboard is the   34._____
    A. plowed   B. mitered
    C. mortise and tenon   D. butt

35. The vehicle used with latex paints is usually   35._____
    A. linseed oil   B. shellac
    C. varnish   D. water

36. *Boxing* of paint refers to the _____ of paints.   36._____
    A. mixing   B. storage   C. use   D. canning

37. When painting wood, nail holes should be puttied   37._____
    A. *before* applying the prime coat
    B. *after* applying the prime coat but before the second coat
    C. *after* applying the second coat but before the third coat
    D. *after* applying the third coat

38. In laying up a brick wall, you find that at the end of the wall there is not enough space for a full brick.   38._____
    You should use a

    A. stretcher   B. bat   C. corbel   D. bull nose

39. Pointing a brick wall is the same as

   A. truing up the wall
   B. topping the wall with a waterproof surface
   C. repairing the mortar joints in the wall
   D. providing a foundation for the wall

40. The pigment MOST often used in a prime coat of paint on steel to prevent rusting is

   A. lampblack   B. calcimine
   C. zinc oxide   D. red lead

41. If you find a co-worker lying unconscious across an electric wire, the FIRST thing you should do is

   A. get him off the wire   B. call the foreman
   C. get a doctor   D. shut off the power

42.

The area of the metal plate shown above, minus the hole area, is MOST NEARLY _____ square inches.

   A. 8.5   B. 8.9   C. 9.4   D. 10.1

43.

The percentage of the above tank that is filled with water is MOST NEARLY

   A. 33   B. 35   C. 37   D. 39

44.

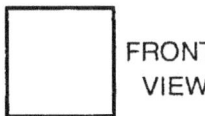

The top and front view of an object are shown above. The right side view will MOST likely look like

A.   B.   C.   D.

45.

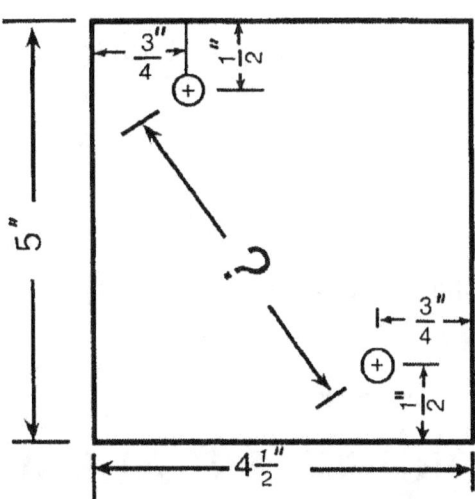

The distance between centers of the holes in the above diagram is MOST NEARLY

A. $4\frac{1}{2}"$ B. 4 3/4"   C. 5"   D. $5\frac{1}{4}"$

Questions 46-48.

DIRECTIONS: Questions 46 through 48, inclusive, are to be answered in accordance with the paragraph below.

A steam heating system with steam having a pressure of less than 10 pounds is called a low-pressure system. The majority of steam-heating systems are of this type. The steam may be provided by low-pressure boilers installed expressly for the purpose, or it may be gener-

ated in boilers at a higher pressure and reduced in pressure before admitted to the heating mains. In other instances, it may be possible to use exhaust steam which has been made to run engines and other machines and which still contains enough heat to be utilized in the heating system. The first case represents the system of heating used in the ordinary residence or other small building; the other two represent the systems of heating employed in industrial buildings where a power plant is installed for general power purposes.

46. According to the above paragraph, whether or not a steam heating system is considered a low pressure system is determined by the pressure

    A. generated by the boiler
    B. in the heating main
    C. at the inlet side of the reducing valve
    D. of the exhaust

47. According to the above paragraph, steam used for heating is sometimes obtained from steam

    A. generated principally to operate machinery
    B. exhausted from larger boilers
    C. generated at low pressure and brought up to high pressure before being used
    D. generated by engines other than boilers

48. As used in the above paragraph, the word *expressly* means

    A. rapidly
    B. specifically
    C. usually
    D. mainly

49. Of the following words, the one that is CORRECTLY spelled is

    A. suficient
    B. sufficiant
    C. sufficient
    D. suficiant

50. Of the following words, the one that is CORRECTLY spelled is

    A. fairly
    B. fairley
    C. farely
    D. fairlie

KEY (CORRECT ANSWERS)

1. B	11. B	21. C	31. B	41. D
2. A	12. D	22. C	32. A	42. B
3. A	13. D	23. B	33. D	43. D
4. C	14. B	24. A	34. B	44. A
5. C	15. C	25. C	35. D	45. C
6. C	16. C	26. C	36. A	46. B
7. B	17. B	27. B	37. B	47. A
8. A	18. D	28. B	38. B	48. B
9. C	19. B	29. A	39. C	49. C
10. B	20. A	30. B	40. D	50. A

EXAMINATION SECTION
TEST 1

DIRECTIONS: Each question or incomplete statement is followed by several suggested answers or completions. Select the one that BEST answers the question or completes the statement. *PRINT THE LETTER OF THE CORRECT ANSWER IN THE SPACE AT THE RIGHT.*

1. The composition of plumber's solder for wiping is APPROXIMATELY (ratio of tin to lead) 1.____

    A. 40-60 B. 50-50 C. 60-40 D. 70-30

2. A device used to lift sewage to the level of a sewer from a floor below the sewer grade is known as a(n) 2.____

    A. elevator B. ejector C. sump D. conveyer

3. A check valve in a piping system will 3.____

    A. permit excessive pressures in a boiler
    B. eliminate water hammer
    C. permit water to flow in only one direction
    D. control the rate of flow of water

4. The chemical MOST frequently used to clean drains clogged with grease is 4.____

    A. muriatic acid B. soda ash
    C. ammonia D. caustic soda

5. To test for leaks in a newly installed C.I. waste stack, 5.____

    A. oil of peppermint is poured into the top of the stack
    B. smoke under pressure is pumped into the stack
    C. a water meter is used to measure the water flow
    D. dye is placed in the system at the top of the stack

6. When installing a catch basin, the outlet should be located 6.____

    A. at the same level as the inlet
    B. above the inlet
    C. below the inlet
    D. at the invert

7. The copper float in a low down water tank is perforated so that water enters the ball. As a result, the tank will 7.____

    A. flush once, and then will not operate again
    B. not flush at all
    C. not flush completely
    D. continue to flush, but water will be wasted

8. If water leaks from the stem of a faucet when the faucet is opened, the _____ should be 8.____

    A. faucet; replaced B. cap nut; rethreaded
    C. seat; reground D. packing; replaced

15

9. In a hot water heating system, it may be necessary to *bleed* radiators to

   A. relieve high steam pressure
   B. permit entrapped, air to escape
   C. allow condensate to return to the boiler
   D. drain off waste water

10. When painting raw wood, puttying of nail holes should be done

    A. 24 hours before the prime coat
    B. immediately before the prime coat
    C. after the prime coat and before the second coat
    D. after the second coat and before the finish

11. In general, the one of the following that will dry *tack free* in the SHORTEST time is

    A. lacquer   B. varnish   C. enamel   D. oil paint

12. The *vehicle* MOST frequently used in paints for exterior wood surfaces is

    A. white lead   B. linseed oil
    C. japan   D. varnish

13. Painting of an interior plastered wall is usually delayed until the plaster is dry. If this practice is NOT followed, the paint might

    A. chalk   B. fade   C. run   D. blister

14. A *sealer* applied over knots and pitch streaks to prevent *bleeding* through paint is

    A. shellac   B. lacquer
    C. coal tar   D. carnauba wax

15. Painting of outside steel in near freezing (32° F) weather is poor practice MAINLY because

    A. the paint will not dry properly
    B. ice will form in the thinner
    C. more paint is required
    D. paint fumes are dangerous

16. When repainting exterior woodwork that has a glossy finish, good adhesion of paint is BEST obtained by first

    A. *washing* the work with diluted lye
    B. *dulling* the work with sandpaper
    C. *warming* the work with an electric heater
    D. *roughening* the work with a rasp

17. The one of the following methods of cleaning steelwork prior to painting that is NOT commonly used on exterior work, such as bridges, is

    A. sandblasting   B. flame cleaning
    C. wire brushing   D. pickling

18. When spraying oil paints, the type of gun and nozzle preferred is a _____ feed gun, _____ mix nozzle.

   A. pressure; internal
   B. pressure, external
   C. syphon; internal
   D. syphon; external

19. When opening a bag of cement, you find that the cement is lumpy.
    The cement should be

   A. discarded and not used at all
   B. crushed before placing in the mixer
   C. used as is since the mixer will grind it
   D. well mixed with water and stored overnight before using

20. A 1:2:4 concrete mix by volume is specified.
    If 6 cubic feet of cement is to be used in the mix, the volume of sand to use is, in cubic feet,

   A. 3   B. 6   C. 12   D. 24

21. Honeycombing in concrete is BEST prevented by

   A. increasing water-cement ratio
   B. heating concrete in cold weather
   C. using mechanical vibrators
   D. adding calcium chloride

22. When a lightweight concrete is required, the one of the following that is COMMONLY used as an aggregate is

   A. gravel   B. brick chips   C. stone   D. cinders

23. A rubbed finish on concrete is USUALLY obtained by use of a

   A. carborundum brick
   B. garnet sanding belt
   C. fibre brush and wax
   D. pad of steel wool

24. A copper strip is frequently embedded in the concrete across a construction joint in a concrete wall.
    The purpose of this is to

   A. make a watertight joint
   B. bond the two parts of the wall together
   C. prevent unequal settlement
   D. retard temperature cracking

25. In brickwork laid in common bond, a header course USUALLY occurs in every _____ course.

   A. 2nd   B. 4th   C. 6th   D. 8th

26. Pointing of brickwork refers to

   A. cutting brick to fit
   B. patching mortar joints
   C. attaching brick veneer
   D. arranging brick in an arch

27. Furring is applied to brick walls to

   A. strengthen the wall
   B. waterproof the wall
   C. provide ventilation to prevent condensation
   D. provide a base for lathing

28. The FIRST coat in plaster work is *scratched* in order to

   A. remove excess plaster
   B. smooth the base for the second coat
   C. provide a bond for the second coat
   D. strengthen the base coat

29. An alloy used where resistance to corrosion is important is

   A. tungsten   B. mild steel   C. monel   D. tin

30. The size of iron pipe is given in terms of its nominal

   A. weight   B. inside diameter
   C. outside diameter   D. wall thickness

31. When preparing surfaces to be soldered, the FIRST step is

   A. tinning   B. sweating   C. heating   D. cleaning

32. To test for leaks in an acetylene torch, it is BEST that one use

   A. soapy water   B. a match
   C. a gas with a strong odor   D. a pressure gauge

33. One advantage of using a Pittsburgh lock seam when joining two pieces of sheet metal is that, once formed in the shop, it may be assembled anywhere with a

   A. hickey   B. swage   C. template   D. mallet

34. White cast iron is

   A. hard and brittle   B. hard and ductile
   C. ductile and malleable   D. brittle and malleable

35. The gage used for measuring copper wire is

   A. U.S. Standard   B. Stubbs
   C. Washburn and Moen   D. Brown and Sharpe

36. The BEST flux to use when soldering copper wires in an electric circuit is

   A. sal ammoniac   B. zinc chloride
   C. rosin   D. borax

37. The spark test, to determine the approximate composition of an unknown metal, is made by

   A. holding the metal against a grinding wheel
   B. striking flint on the unknown metal
   C. connecting wires from a source of electric power to the metal and striking an arc with a bare wire
   D. heating with an oxyacetylene torch

38. The one of the following metals that is MOST commonly used for bearings is 38.____
   A. duraluminum   B. brass   C. babbit   D. lead

39. A *tailstock* is found on a 39.____
   A. drill press   B. shaper   C. planer   D. lathe

40. The BEST lubricant to use when cutting screw threads in steel is 40.____
   A. naphtha   B. 3-in-1 oil
   C. lard oil   D. linseed oil

41. When a high speed cutting tool is required, the tip is frequently made of 41.____
   A. carborundum   B. tungsten carbide
   C. bronze   D. vanadium

42. A nut is turned on a 3/4"-10 bolt. 42.____
    When the nut is turned five complete turns on this bolt, the distance it moves along the bolt
   A. depends on the type of thread   B. is 0.2 inches
   C. is 0.375 inches   D. is 0.5 inches

43. Of the following, the STRONGEST screw thread form is the 43.____
   A. Whitworth   B. Acme
   C. National Standard D. V

44. *Knurling* refers to 44.____
   A. rolling depressions in a fixed pattern on a cylindrical surface
   B. turning between centers on a lathe
   C. making deep cuts in a flat plate with a milling machine
   D. drilling matching holes in bolt and nut for a cotter pin

45. A special device used to guide the drill as well as to hold the work when drilling is known as a 45.____
   A. dolly   B. jig   C. chuck   D. collet

46. Tools that have a *Morse taper* would be used on a 46.____
   A. milling machine   B. shaper
   C. planer   D. drill press

47. When tapping a blind hole in a plate, the FIRST tap to use is a 47.____
   A. plug   B. bottoming   C. lead   D. taper

48. An important safety practice to remember when cutting a rivet with a chisel is to wear 48.____
   A. leather gloves   B. steel toe shoes
   C. cup goggles   D. a hard hat

49. Electricians working around *live wires* should wear gloves made of 49.____

   A. asbestos   B. metal mesh   C. leather   D. rubber

50. Storage of oily rags presents a safety hazard because of possible 50.____

   A. fire
   C. attraction of rats
   B. poisonous flames
   D. leakage of oil

KEY (CORRECT ANSWERS)

1. A	11. A	21. C	31. D	41. B
2. B	12. B	22. D	32. A	42. D
3. C	13. D	23. A	33. D	43. B
4. D	14. A	24. A	34. A	44. A
5. B	15. A	25. C	35. B	45. B
6. C	16. B	26. B	36. C	46. D
7. D	17. D	27. D	37. A	47. D
8. D	18. A	28. C	38. C	48. C
9. B	19. A	29. C	39. D	49. D
10. C	20. C	30. B	40. C	50. A

TEST 2

DIRECTIONS: Each question or incomplete statement is followed by several suggested answers or completions. Select the one that BEST answers the question or completes the statement. *PRINT THE LETTER OF THE CORRECT ANSWER IN THE SPACE AT THE RIGHT.*

1. *Shimmying* of the front wheels of a truck is MOST frequently caused by 1.____

    A. worn front brake drums
    B. a worn differential gear
    C. a loose steering gear
    D. a dead shock absorber

2. The MOST important reason for maintaining correct air pressure in all tires of a truck is to 2.____

    A. prevent the truck from swerving when brakes are applied
    B. permit the truck to stop quicker in an emergency
    C. provide a smoother ride
    D. prevent excessive wear on the tires

3. The oil gage on the dashboard of a truck indicates 3.____

    A. the amount of oil in the pan
    B. the pressure at which the oil is being pumped
    C. if the oil filter is working
    D. the temperature of the oil in the motor

4. An unbalanced wheel on a truck is corrected by 4.____

    A. bending the rim slightly
    B. adjusting the king pin
    C. changing the ratio of caster to camber
    D. adding small weights to the rim

5. A cold motor on a truck should be warmed up in wintertime by 5.____

    A. turning on the heater and pouring warm water into the radiator
    B. allowing the motor to idle for a few minutes
    C. racing the motor
    D. alternately pressing the gas pedal to the floor and releasing it

6. The brake pedal on a truck goes to the floorboard when pushed. 6.____
The one of the following that would cause this condition is

    A. air in the hydraulic system
    B. wet brakes
    C. excessive fluid in the cylinders
    D. a loose backing plate

7. The ammeter of a truck indicates no charge during operation even though the battery is 7.____
run down. To find the fault, the generator field terminal is grounded. The ammeter now shows a charge. The part that is defective is the

    A. generator field coil
    B. armature
    C. brushes
    D. voltage regulator

21

8. The part used to control the ratio of air and gasoline in a truck engine is the

   A. bogie B. filter C. carburetor D. pump

9. The MAIN purpose of a vacuum booster on a truck engine is to

   A. increase the manifold vacuum
   B. assist windshield wiper operation
   C. provide a steadier fuel flow
   D. govern engine speed

10. The purpose of grounding the frame of an electric motor is to

    A. prevent excessive vibration
    B. eliminate shock hazards
    C. reduce power requirements
    D. prevent overheating

11. The one of the following that is NOT part of an electric motor is a

    A. brush B. rheostat C. pole D. commutator

12. An electrical transformer would be used to

    A. change current from AC to DC
    B. raise or lower the power
    C. raise or lower the voltage
    D. change the frequency

13. The piece of equipment that would be rated in ampere hours is a

    A. storage battery
    B. bus bar
    C. rectifier
    D. capacitor

14. A ballast is a necessity in a(n)

    A. motor generator set
    B. fluorescent lighting system
    C. oil circuit breaker
    D. synchronous converter

15. The power factor in an AC circuit is on when

    A. no current is flowing
    B. the voltage at the source is a minimum
    C. the voltage and current are in phase
    D. there is no load

16.

    Neglecting the internal resistance in the battery, the current flowing through the battery shown in the sketch above is _____ amp.

    A. 3 B. 6 C. 9 D. 12

3 (#2)

17. When excess current flows, a circuit breaker is opened directly by the action of a   17.____

   A. condenser   B. transistor   C. relay   D. solenoid

18. The MAIN purpose of bridging in building floor construction is to   18.____

   A. spread floor loads evenly to joists
   B. reduce the number of joists required
   C. permit use of thinner subflooring
   D. reduce noise passage through floors

19. Of the following, the material MOST commonly used for subflooring is   19.____

   A. rock lath   B. insulation board
   C. plywood   D. transite

20. In connection with stair construction, the one of the following that is LEAST related to the others is   20.____

   A. tread   B. cap   C. nosing   D. riser

21. The type of nail MOST commonly used in flooring is   21.____

   A. common   B. cut   C. brad   D. casing

22. The edge joint of flooring boards is COMMONLY   22.____

   A. mortise and tenon   B. shiplap
   C. half lap   D. tongue and groove

23. The purpose of a ridge board in building construction is to   23.____

   A. locate corners of a building
   B. keep plaster work smooth
   C. support the ends of roof rafters
   D. conceal openings at the eaves

24. To prevent splintering of wood when using an auger bit,   24.____

   A. the bit should be hollow ground
   B. hold the piece of wood in a vise
   C. clamp a piece of scrap wood to the back of the piece being drilled
   D. use a slow speed on the drill press

25. End grain of a post can be MOST easily planed by use of a _____ plane.   25.____

   A. rafter   B. jack   C. fore   D. block

26. A butt gauge is used when   26.____

   A. hanging doors   B. laying out stairs
   C. making rafter cuts   D. framing studs

27. The one of the following grades of sandpaper with the FINEST grit is   27.____

   A. 0   B. 2/0   C. 1/2   D. 1

23

28. The sum of the following numbers, 3 7/8, 14 1/4, 6 7/16, 22 3/16, 8 1/2 is

    A. 55 1/16   B. 55 1/8   C. 55 3/16   D. 55 1/4

29. The area of the rectangular field shown in the diagram at the right is, in square feet,
    A. 29,456
    B. 29,626
    C. 29,716
    D. 29,836

    437 FT.

    68 ft

30. The cost of material is approximately 3/8ths of the total cost of a certain job. If the total cost of the job is $127.56, then the cost of material is MOST NEARLY

    A. $47.83   B. $48.24   C. $48.65   D. $49.06

31. A blueprint is drawn to a scale of 1/4" = 1'0". A line on the blueprint that is not dimensioned is measured with a ruler and found to be 3 3/8" long.
    The length represented by this line is

    A. 13'2"   B. 13'4"   C. 13'6"   D. 13'8"

32. A maintainer, in repairing a brick wall, spends one-half hour getting materials, forty-three minutes chipping and cleaning the wall, fifteen minutes mixing the mortar, and one hour and twenty-seven minutes in applying the brick and finishing.
    The total time spent on this repair job is _____ hours _____ minute(s).

    A. 2; 45   B. 2; 50   C. 2; 55   D. 3; 0

33. *Employees are responsible for the good care, proper maintenance, and serviceable condition of property issued or assigned to their use.*
    As used above, *serviceable condition* means MOST NEARLY

    A. capable of being repaired   B. fit for use
    C. ease of handling   D. minimum cost

34. An employee shall be on the alert constantly for potential accident hazards.
    As used above, *potential* means MOST NEARLY

    A. dangerous   B. careless   C. possible   D. frequent

Questions 35-37.

DIRECTIONS: Questions 35 to 37, inclusive, are to be answered in accordance with the following paragraph.

All cement work contracts, more or less, in setting. The contraction in concrete walls and other structures causes fine cracks to develop at regular intervals. The tendency to contract increases in direct proportion to the quantity of cement in the concrete. A rich mixture will contract more than a lean mixture. A concrete wall, which has been made of a very lean mixture and which has been built by filling only about one foot in depth of concrete in the form each day will frequently require close inspection to reveal the cracks.

35. According to the above paragraph,

    A. shrinkage seldom occurs in concrete
    B. shrinkage occurs only in certain types of concrete
    C. by placing concrete at regular intervals, shrinkage may be avoided
    D. it is impossible to prevent shrinkage

36. According to the above paragraph, the one of the factors which reduces shrinkage in concrete is the

    A. volume of concrete in wall
    B. height of each day's pour
    C. length of wall
    D. length and height of wall

37. According to the above paragraph, a rich mixture

    A. pours the easiest
    B. shows the largest amount of cracks
    C. is low in cement content
    D. need not be inspected since cracks are few

Questions 38-39.

DIRECTIONS: Questions 38 and 39 are to be answered in accordance with the following paragraph.

Painting is done to preserve surfaces, and unless the surface is properly prepared, good preservation will not be possible. Apply paint only to clean dry surfaces. After a surface has been scaled, which means that all loose paint and rust are removed by chipping, scraping, and wire brushing, be sure all dust and dirt are completely removed.

38. According to the above paragraph, the MAIN purpose of painting a wall is to _____ the wall.

    A. clean   B. waterproof
    C. protect   D. remove dust from

39. According to the above paragraph,

    A. chipping, scraping, and wire brushing are the only methods permitted for cleaning surfaces
    B. painting is effective only when the surface is clean
    C. scaling refers only to the removal of rust
    D. paint may be applied on wet surfaces

40. The order in which the dimensions of stock are listed on a bill of materials is

    A. thickness, length, and width   B. thickness, width, and length
    C. width, length, and thickness   D. length, thickness, and width

41. The glue that will BEST withstand extreme exposure to moisture and water is _____ glue.

    A. polyvinyl
    B. resorcinol
    C. powdered resin
    D. protein

42. Four board feet of lumber, listed at $350.00 per M, will cost

    A. $3.50 B. $1.40 C. $1.30 D. $4.00

43. The cap iron or chip breaker stiffens the plane iron and

    A. protects the cutting edge
    B. curls the shaving
    C. regulates the thickness of the shaving
    D. reduces mouth gap

44. Coping-saw blades have teeth shaped like those on a _____ saw.

    A. dovetail B. crosscut C. back D. rip

45. Of the following, the claw hammer that is BEST suited for general use in a woodworking shop is the _____ claw.

    A. straight
    B. bell-faced curved
    C. plain-faced curved
    D. adze eye curved

46. The natural binder which cements wood fibers together and makes wood solid is

    A. cellulose
    B. lignin
    C. alpha-cellulose
    D. trichocarpa

47. The plane that is BEST suited for trimming the bottom of a dado or lap joint is the _____ plane.

    A. block B. router C. rabbet D. core-box

48. Brads are fasteners that are similar to _____ nails.

    A. escutcheon
    B. box
    C. finishing
    D. duplex head

49. The plane in which the plane iron is inserted with its bevel in the up position is the _____ plane.

    A. fore B. rabbet C. block D. circular

50. Coating materials used to protect wood against fire USUALLY contain a water soluble fire-retardant such as

    A. ammonium chloride
    B. sodium perborate
    C. sodium silicate
    D. sal soda

KEY (CORRECT ANSWERS)

1. C	11. B	21. B	31. C	41. B
2. D	12. C	22. D	32. C	42. B
3. B	13. A	23. C	33. B	43. B
4. D	14. B	24. C	34. C	44. D
5. B	15. C	25. D	35. D	45. B
6. A	16. A	26. A	36. B	46. B
7. D	17. D	27. B	37. B	47. B
8. C	18. A	28. D	38. C	48. C
9. B	19. C	29. C	39. B	49. C
10. B	20. B	30. A	40. B	50. C

EXAMINATION SECTION
TEST 1

DIRECTIONS: Each question or incomplete statement is followed by several suggested answers or completions. Select the one that BEST answers the question or completes the statement. *PRINT THE LETTER OF THE CORRECT ANSWER IN THE SPACE AT THE RIGHT.*

1. Asbestos was used as a covering on electrical wires to provide protection from   1.____

   A. high voltage
   B. high temperature
   C. water damage
   D. electrolysis

2. The rating term *240 volts, 10 H.P.* would be PROPERLY used to describe a   2.____

   A. transformer
   B. storage battery
   C. motor
   D. rectifier

3. Rigid steel conduit used for the protection of electrical wiring is GENERALLY either galvanized or enameled both inside and out in order to   3.____

   A. prevent damage to the wire insulation
   B. make threading of the conduit easier
   C. prevent corrosion of the conduit
   D. make the conduit easier to handle

4. BX is COMMONLY used to indicate   4.____

   A. rigid conduit without wires
   B. flexible conduit without wires
   C. insulated wires covered with flexible steel armor
   D. insulated wires covered with a non-metallic covering

5. If a test lamp does not light when placed in series with a fuse and an appropriate battery, it is a GOOD indication that the fuse   5.____

   A. is open-circuited
   B. is short-circuited
   C. is in operating condition
   D. has zero resistance

6. Of the following, the SIMPLEST wood joint to make is a   6.____

   A. half lap joint
   B. mortise and tenon
   C. butt joint
   D. multiple dovetail

7. To accurately cut a number of lengths of wood at an angle of 45 degrees, it would be BEST to use a   7.____

   A. protractor
   B. mitre-box
   C. triangle
   D. square

8. The soffit of a beam is the   8.____

   A. span   B. side   C. bottom   D. top

29

9. A nail set is a tool used for

   A. straightening bent nails
   B. cutting nails to specified size
   C. sinking a nail head in wood
   D. measuring nail size

10. It is UNLAWFUL to

    A. use wooden lath
    B. have ceiling lath run in one direction only
    C. break joints when using wood lath
    D. run wood lath through from room to room

11. A concrete mix for a construction job requires a certain ratio of cement, water, sand, and small stones.
    The MOST serious error in mixing would be to use 20% too much

    A. sand   B. water
    C. small stones   D. mixing time

12. Impurities in a mortar which may seriously affect its strength are MOST likely to enter the mortar with the

    A. mixing water   B. sand
    C. lime   D. gypsum

13. One ADVANTAGE of using plywood instead of boards for concrete forms is that plywood

    A. needs no bracing
    B. does not split easily
    C. sticks less to concrete
    D. insulates concrete against freezing

14. Concrete will crack MOST easily when it is subject to

    A. compression   B. bearing
    C. bonding   D. tension

15. Where a smooth dense finish is desired for a concrete surface, it will BEST be produced by using a

    A. wood float   B. level
    C. steel trowel   D. vibrator

16. Sewer gas is prevented from backing up through a fixture by a

    A. water trap   B. vent pipe
    C. check valve   D. float valve

17. Packing is used in an adjustable water valve MAINLY to

    A. make it air-tight
    B. prevent mechanical wear
    C. regulate the water pressure
    D. make it water-tight

18. Good practice requires that the end of a piece of water pipe be reamed to remove the inside burr after it has been cut to length.
The PURPOSE of the reaming is to

   A. finish the pipe accurately to length
   B. make the threading easier
   C. avoid cutting of the workers' hands
   D. allow free passage for the flow of water

19. The MAIN reason for pitching a steam pipe in a heating system is to

   A. prevent accumulation of condensed steam
   B. present a smaller radiating surface
   C. facilitate repairs
   D. reduce friction in the pipe

20. When fitting pipe together, poor alignment of pipe and fittings would MOST likely result in

   A. leaky joints
   B. cracking of the pipe on expansion
   C. formation of hot spots
   D. cracking of the pipe on contraction

21. Roofing nails are GENERALLY

   A. brass plated   B. galvanized
   C. cement coated   D. nickel plated

22. Specifications for a roofing job call for 3 *lbs. sheet lead*. This means that each sheet SHOULD weigh 3 lbs. per

   A. square inch   B. square foot
   C. square yard   D. sheet

23. The MAIN reason for using flashing at the intersection of different roof planes is to

   A. increase the durability of the shingles
   B. simplify the installation of the shingles
   C. waterproof the roof
   D. improve the appearance of the roof

24. Of the following roofing materials, the one that is MOST frequently used in *built-up* roofs is

   A. asbestos shingles   B. three-ply felt
   C. sheet copper   D. wood sheathing

25. As used in roofing, *a square* refers to

   A. a tool for lining up the roofing with the eaves of the house
   B. one hundred square feet of roofing
   C. one hundred shingles of roofing
   D. one hundred pounds of roofing

26. In the process of replacing a pane of window glass, the old putty should be scraped off the window sash and the wood surfaces then primed with

    A. resin oil
    B. shellac
    C. linseed oil
    D. enamel

27. The LARGEST available size of glazier's points is number

    A. 3
    B. 1
    C. 0
    D. 000

28. The purpose of priming wood window sash before applying putty and glass is to prevent the

    A. putty from absorbing moisture from the wood
    B. putty from staining the wood
    C. wood from absorbing the oils from the putty
    D. natural wood resins from making the putty brittle

29. When hard, dry putty must be removed from a wood window frame in order to put in a new pane of glass, the BEST tool with which to do this job is a

    A. screwdriver
    B. putty knife
    C. wide wood chisel
    D. pocket knife

30. Before repainting a wood surface on which the old paint film has developed some wrinkling, the MOST appropriate treatment for the wood surface is a

    A. thorough scraping
    B. light shellacking
    C. wash-down with dilute muriatic acid
    D. rubbing down of the wrinkles with fairly coarse sand-paper

31. A paint that is characterized by its ability to dry to an especially smooth, hard, glossy or semi-glossy finish is called a(n)

    A. primer
    B. sealer
    C. glaze
    D. enamel

32. The BEST thinner for varnish is

    A. gasoline
    B. turpentine
    C. kerosene
    D. water

33. To get a good paint job on a new plaster wall, one should make certain that the

    A. wall is thoroughly dry before painting
    B. base coat is much darker than the finishing coat
    C. wall has been roughened enough to make the paint stick
    D. plaster has not completely set

34. In a three-coat plaster job, the brown coat is applied

    A. before the scratch coat has set
    B. immediately after the scratch coat
    C. after the scratch coat has set and partially dried
    D. after the scratch coat has thoroughly dried out

35. Plaster which has sand as an aggregate, when compared with plaster which has a lightweight aggregate, is

   A. a better sound absorber
   B. a better insulator
   C. less likely to crack under a sharp blow
   D. cheaper

36. One form of metal lath comes in sheets 27" x 96".
    The number of sheets required to cover 20 square yards without overlap is

   A. 9   B. 10   C. 11   D. 12

37. When nailing gypsum board lath to studs or furring strips, the nailing should be started_____ of the board.

   A. along the top   B. along the bottom
   C. at the center   D. at one end

38. A wooden mortar box for slaking lime is lined with sheet iron.
    Of the following, the GREATEST advantage of the lining is that

   A. a better grade putty is produced
   B. the box is easier to clean
   C. it makes the box water-tight
   D. it prevents burning of the wood

39. The Building Code requires that water used in plastering MUST

   A. be perfectly clear in color
   B. not have any rust in it
   C. be fit for drinking
   D. not be fluoridated

40. In order to prevent thin sheet metal from buckling when riveting it to an angle iron, the BEST procedure is to

   A. start riveting at one end of the sheet and work toward the other end
   B. start riveting at both ends of the sheet and work in toward the center
   C. install alternate rivets working in one direction, and then fill in the remaining rivets working in the other direction
   D. start riveting in the center of the joint, working out in both directions

KEY (CORRECT ANSWERS)

1. B	11. B	21. B	31. D
2. C	12. B	22. B	32. B
3. C	13. B	23. C	33. A
4. C	14. D	24. B	34. C
5. A	15. C	25. B	35. D
6. C	16. A	26. C	36. B
7. B	17. D	27. C	37. C
8. C	18. D	28. C	38. B
9. C	19. A	29. C	39. C
10. D	20. A	30. D	40. D

TEST 2

DIRECTIONS: Each question or incomplete statement is followed by several suggested answers or completions. Select the one that BEST answers the question or completes the statement. *PRINT THE LETTER OF THE CORRECT ANSWER IN THE SPACE AT THE RIGHT.*

1. A drill bit measures .625 inches.   1.____
   The FRACTIONAL EQUIVALENT, in inches, is

   A. 9/16 B. 5/8 C. 11/16 D. 3/4

2. The number of cubic yards of sand required to fill a bin measuring 12 feet by 6 feet by 4 feet is MOST NEARLY   2.____

   A. 8 B. 11 C. 48 D. 96

3. Assume that you are assigned to put down floor tiles in a room measuring 8 feet by 10 feet. Individual tiles measure 9 inches by 9 inches.   3.____
   The total number of floor tiles required to cover the entire floor is MOST NEARLY

   A. 107 B. 121 C. 144 D. 160

4. Lumber is usually sold by the board foot, and a board foot is defined as a board one foot square and one inch thick.   4.____
   If the price of one board foot of lumber is 18 cents and you need 20 feet of lumber 6 inches wide and 1 inch thick, the cost of the 20 feet of the lumber is

   A. $1.80 B. $2.40 C. $3.60 D. $4.80

5. For a certain plumbing repair job, you need three lengths of pipe, 12 1/4 inches, 6 1/2 inches, and 8 5/8 inches.   5.____
   If you cut these three lengths from the same piece of pipe, which is 36 inches long, and each cut consumes 1/8 inch of pipe, the length of pipe REMAINING after you have cut out your three pieces should be _____ inches.

   A. 7 1/4 B. 7 7/8 C. 8 1/4 D. 8 7/8

6. Glazier points are small pieces of galvanized metal often having the shape of a(n)   6.____

   A. circle B. ellipse C. square D. triangle

7. Putty that is too stiff is made workable by adding   7.____

   A. gasoline B. linseed oil
   C. water D. lacquer thinner

8. Soap is applied to wood screws before they are used in order to   8.____

   A. prevent rust
   B. make a tight fit
   C. make insertion easier
   D. prevent screws from loosening after insertion

9. A method sometimes used to prevent a pipe from buckling during a bending operation is to   9.____

35

A. bend the pipe very quickly
B. keep the seam of the pipe on the outside of the bend
C. nick the pipe at the center of the bend
D. pack the inside of the pipe with sand

10. Rubber gaskets are frequently placed between the faces of the flanges when making up a flanged joint in a pipe line in order to

A. prevent corrosion of the machined faces
B. permit full tightening of the flange bolts without danger of thread stripping
C. eliminate the necessity for accurate alignment of the pipe
D. make a tight joint

11. A parapet is the

A. stepping out of successive courses of brickwork
B. continuation of a wall above the roof line
C. wall enclosing stairs that lead to the roof
D. portion of an exterior wall below a window

12. The process of removing the insulation from a wire is called

A. braiding   B. skinning   C. sweating   D. tinning

13. The process of making fresh concrete watertight, durable, and strong after it has been poured is called

A. air-entraining
B. finishing
C. curing
D. accelerating

14. A mixture of cement, sand, and water is called

A. hydrated lime
B. plain concrete
C. hydrated cement
D. mortar

15. The *grip* applied to a pipe with gas pliers is increased by using pliers with

A. longer handles
B. larger jaws
C. thicker handles
D. larger teeth

16. Those materials which are added to a paint vehicle to regulate its consistency and thus increase its spreading power and facilitate its application are called

A. driers
B. thinners
C. extenders
D. oxidents

17. The fitting which usually is easiest to disconnect FIRST when disassembling a piping run is a(n)

A. cross
B. union
C. return bend
D. elbow

18. For convenience in case of future repairs to a long pipe line, it is DESIRABLE to fit the pipe together with several

A. street ells
B. elbows
C. return bends
D. unions

19. If four pipes are to be connected into each other at a common point, it would be NECESSARY to use a(n)

   A. tee fitting B. street ell
   C. cross D. offset

20. The BEST of the following tools to use for cutting off a piece of single conductor #6 rubber insulated lead covered cable is a

   A. pair of electrician's pliers
   B. hacksaw
   C. hammer and cold chisel
   D. lead knife

21. One ADVANTAGE of rubber insulation is that it

   A. does not deteriorate with age
   B. is able to withstand high temperature
   C. does not absorb much moisture
   D. is not damaged by oil

22. The SIMPLEST device for interrupting an overloaded electrical circuit is a

   A. fuse B. relay
   C. capacitor D. choke-coil

23. Reinforced concrete USUALLY means concrete that has been strengthened by use of

   A. additional cement B. steel bars
   C. extra heavy gravel D. high strength cement

24. A VERTICAL wood member in the wall of a wood frame house is known as a

   A. stringer B. ridge member
   C. stud D. header

25. A riser is GENERALLY a pipe run which is

   A. horizontal B. curved
   C. vertical D. at a 45-degree angle

26. A standard pipe thread DIFFERS from a standard screw thread in that the pipe thread

   A. is tapered
   B. is deeper
   C. requires no lubrication when cutting
   D. has the same pitch for any diameter of pipe

27. The material which is LEAST likely to be found in use as the outer covering of rubber insulated wires or cables is

   A. cotton B. varnished cambric
   C. lead D. neoprene

28. In measuring to determine the size of a standard insulated conductor, the PROPER place to use the wire gauge is on

A. the insulation
B. the outer covering
C. the stranded conductor
D. one strand of the conductor

29. Rubber insulation on an electrical conductor would MOST quickly be damaged by continuous contact with

A. acid B. water C. oil D. alkali

30. If a fuse clip becomes hot under normal circuit load, the MOST probable cause is that the

A. clip makes poor contact with the fuse ferrule
B. circuit wires are too small
C. current rating of the fuse is too high
D. voltage rating of the fuse is too low

31. If the input to a 10 to 1 step-down transformer is 15 amperes at 2400 volts, the secondary output would be NEAREST to _____ amperes at _____ volts.

A. 1.5; 24,000
B. 150; 240
C. 1.5; 240
D. 150; 24,000

32. The resistance of a copper wire to the flow of electricity _____ as the _____ of the wire _____.

A. increases; diameter; increases
B. decreases; diameter; decreases
C. decreases; length; increases
D. increases; length; increases

33. Where galvanized steel conduit is used, the PRIMARY purpose of the galvanizing is to

A. increase mechanical strength
B. retard rusting
C. provide a good surface for painting
D. provide good electrical contact for grounding

34. The lamps used for station and tunnel lighting in the subways are generally operated at slightly less than their rated voltage.
The LOGICAL reason for this is to

A. prevent overloading of circuits
B. increase the life of the lamps
C. decrease glare
D. obtain a more even distribution of light

35. The CORRECT method of measuring the power taken by an a.c. electric motor is to use a

A. wattmeter
B. voltmeter and an ammeter
C. power factor meter
D. tachometer

36. Wood ladders should NOT be painted because the paint

    A. may deteriorate the wood
    B. makes the ladders slippery
    C. is inflammable
    D. may cover cracks or defects

37. Goggles would be LEAST necessary when

    A. recharging soda-acid fire extinguishers
    B. chipping stone
    C. putting electrolyte into an Edison battery
    D. scraping rubber insulation from a wire

38. The number and type of precautions to be taken on a job generally depend LEAST on the

    A. nature of the job
    B. length of time the job is expected to last
    C. kind of tools and materials being used
    D. location of the work

39. When training workers in the use of tools and equipment, safety precautions related to their use should be FIRST mentioned

    A. in the introductory training session before the workers begin to use the equipment or tools
    B. during training sessions when workers practice operating the tools or equipment
    C. after the workers are qualified to use the equipment in their daily tasks
    D. when an agency safety bulletin related to the tools and equipment is received

40. Many portable electric power tools, such as electric drills, have a third conductor in the power lead which is used to connect the case of the tool to a grounded part of the electric outlet.
    The reason for this extra conductor is to

    A. have a spare wire in case one power wire should break
    B. strengthen the power lead so it cannot easily be damaged
    C. prevent the user of the tool from being shocked
    D. enable the tool to be used for long periods of time without overheating

KEY (CORRECT ANSWERS)

1.	B	11.	B	21.	C	31.	B
2.	B	12.	B	22.	A	32.	D
3.	C	13.	C	23.	B	33.	B
4.	A	14.	D	24.	C	34.	B
5.	C	15.	A	25.	C	35.	A
6.	D	16.	B	26.	A	36.	D
7.	B	17.	B	27.	B	37.	D
8.	C	18.	D	28.	D	38.	B
9.	D	19.	C	29.	C	39.	A
10.	D	20.	B	30.	A	40.	C

EXAMINATION SECTION
TEST 1

DIRECTIONS: Each question or incomplete statement is followed by several suggested answers or completions. Select the one that BEST answers the question or completes the statement. *PRINT THE LETTER OF THE CORRECT ANSWER IN THE SPACE AT THE RIGHT.*

1. A shrink fitted collar is to be removed from a shaft. One good way to do this would be to drive out the shaft after _____ collar.

    A. *chilling* only the
    B. *chilling* both the shaft and
    C. *heating* only the
    D. *heating* both the shaft and

    1.____

2. It is CORRECT to say that

    A. a standard brick weighs about 8 lbs.
    B. the dimensions of a common brick are 8" x 3 3/4" x 2 1/4"
    C. vertical joints in a brick wall are called bed joints
    D. in laying bricks the head joints should be slushed with mortar

    2.____

3. A snail pump impeller is checked for static balance by

    A. running the pump at high speed and listening for rubs
    B. mounting it on parallel and level knife edges and noting if it turns
    C. weighing it and comparing the weight against the original weight
    D. putting it on a lathe to see if it runs true

    3.____

4. The sum of the following dimensions: 3' x 2 1/4", 8 7/8", 2'6 3/8", 2'9 3/4", and 1'0" is

    A. 16'7 1/4"   B. 10'7 1/4"   C. 10'3 1/4"   D. 9'3 1/4"

    4.____

5. A requisition for nails was worded as follows: *100 lbs., 10d, 3 inch, common wive nails, galvanized.*
   The UNNECESSARY information in this requisition is

    A. 100 lbs.   B. common   C. galvanized   D. 3 inch

    5.____

6. Electric arc welding is COMMONLY done by the use of _____ voltage and _____ amperage.

    A. *low; high*   B. *high; high*
    C. *high; low*   D. *low; low*

    6.____

7. A GOOD principle for you to follow after teaching a maintenance procedure to a new helper is to

    A. tell him that you expect him to make many mistakes at first
    B. observe his work procedure and point out any errors he may make
    C. have him write out the procedure from memory
    D. assume he knows the procedure if he asks no questions

    7.____

8. Multiple threads are used on the stems of some large valves to

   A. reduce the effort required to open the valve
   B. prevent binding of the valve stem
   C. secure faster opening and closing of the valve
   D. decrease the length of stem travel

9. After the base plate of a new machine has been fitted over the foundation bolts, it should be leveled by

   A. inserting steel shims under the plate
   B. chipping the high spots off the floor
   C. using thin cement grout under the plate
   D. grinding down the high spots on the base plate

10. In nixing concrete by hand, the materials are first thoroughly mixed dry and then mixed with water. This is a good procedure because it

    A. caves cement
    B. reduces the amount of water required
    C. avoids settling of the aggregate
    D. properly coats the aggregate with the cement

11. A revolution counter applied to the end of a rotating shaft reads 100 when a stopwatch is started and 850 after 90 seconds.
    The shaft is rotating at a speed of _____ rpm.

    A. 500   B. 633   C. 750   D. 950

12. If a kink develops in a wire rope, it would be BEST to

    A. hammer out the kink with a lead hammer
    B. straighten out the kink by putting it in a vise and applying sufficient pressure
    C. discard the portion of the rope containing the kink
    D. keep the rope in use and allow the kink to work itself out

13. Steel pipe posts have been placed into prepared holes in concrete.
    To properly secure the posts, they should be caulked inplace with

    A. molten lead   B. cement mortar
    C. oakum   D. hot pitch

14. The PRINCIPAL reason for grounding of electrical equipment is to

    A. save power   B. guard against shock
    C. prevent open circuits   D. prevent short circuits

15. A spirit level has been dropped and a deep indentation made in the wood.
    The BEST thing to do is to

    A. ignore the incident if the bubbles were not broken
    B. sand down the surface to remove the indentation
    C. get a new level
    D. test the level

16. A strike plate is MOST closely associated with a

    A. lock
    B. sash weight
    C. hinge
    D. door check

17. You receive a special assignment from your superior calling for the use of a type of wood which in your opinion is not suitable for the job.
    You should

    A. substitute the wood you believe to be most suitable
    B. carry out the order as received
    C. immediately call this to his attention
    D. consult another maintainer on what to do

18. A motor driven centrifugal pump takes water from a city main and delivers it to the nozzles of a train washing machine. With little change in motor speed or suction pressure, the discharge pressure rises and the flow of cleaning water falls to a trickle.
    The PROBABLE cause is a

    A. failure of the impeller shaft
    B. leak in the piping between the pressure gage point of attachment and the nozzles
    C. blockage of the impeller
    D. blockage between the pressure gage point of attachment and the nozzles

19. A standard hoisting rope size is designated as 6 x 19. This indicates that the rope has

    A. 6 strands, each made of 19 wires
    B. 19 strands, each made of 6 wires
    C. 6 strands of No. 19 gage wire
    D. 19 strands of No. 6 gage wire

20. The two planes which make up the MOST useful combination for general carpentry work are the _____ plane and the _____ plane.

    A. jack; jointer
    B. jack; block
    C. smooth; block
    D. fore; jointer

21. If you were drilling a structural plate and the drill cuttings were in the form of long continuous shavings, you could rightly conclude that the

    A. drill point was too sharp
    B. material being drilled was wrought iron
    C. bearing pressure on the drill was insufficient
    D. drilling was being done correctly

22. Studs and joists for light building construction are USUALLY spaced on _____ inch centers.

    A. 12
    B. 14
    C. 16
    D. 18

23. If power driven rivets are loose, the MOST likely reason would be that the rivets were

    A. too long
    B. too short
    C. driven with high air pressure
    D. overheated

24. If a drawing for a pipe installation is made to a scale of 1 1/2" to the foot, the drawing is said to be one _____ size.

   A. half   B. quarter   C. eighth   D. sixteenth

25. A gear train consists of a driver with 120 teeth, an idler with 60 teeth, and a driven gear with 200 teeth. If the driver rotates at 1500 rpm, the driven gear rotates at _____ rpm.

   A. 225   B. 900   C. 2500   D. 10,000

26. A certain pipe fitting is marked *200 WOG.* This fitting could NOT properly be used in a pipe line for _____ pounds gage maximum.

   A. steam at 200
   B. water at 150
   C. air at 200
   D. oil at 150

27. A file having two *safe* edges is COMMONLY known as a _____ file.

   A. flat   B. mill   C. hand   D. pillar

28. By trial, it is found that by using 2 cubic feet of sand, a 5 cubic foot batch of concrete is produced.
   Using the same proportions, the amount of sand, in cubic feet, required to produce 2 cubic yards of concrete is MOST NEARLY

   A. 7   B. 22   C. 27   D. 45

29. Tooling of the face joints of a brick wall under construction should be done

   A. after the mortar has acquired its initial set
   B. after the entire wall is laid
   C. after the mortar has acquired its final set
   D. as each brick is laid

30. A gland bushing is associated in practice with a(n)

   A. gas engine
   B. electric motor
   C. centrifugal pump
   D. lathe

31. A house drain is successively offset by means of a 1/8 bend, a 1/16 bend, and a 1/32 bend.
   The total angular offset of this line is MOST NEARLY

   A. 34°   B. 39°   C. 68°   D. 79°

32. The flushing mechanism in a low tank water closet is so arranged that a fill tube supplies water from the ball cock to the overflow standpipe for a short interval immediately after the closet is flushed.
   The MAIN reason for this is to

   A. finish cleaning the water passages of the closet
   B. properly seal the ball in its seat
   C. renew the seal in the closet trap
   D. scour the flush tube from the tank to the closet

33. A job calls for the setting of wrought iron pipe sleeves in concrete floor construction for the passage of water risers.
    In order to provide for the passage of a 2" riser, the MINIMUM diameter of the sleeve is

    A. 2 1/2"   B. 3"   C. 4"   D. 5"

34. When applied to lumber, the designation *S4S* means

    A. all sides are rough
    B. all four sides are of the same size
    C. fourth grade lumber
    D. all sides are dressed

35. To guard against accidents in connection with wood scaffolding,

    A. inspect the nailing before the scaffold is loaded
    B. never put a heavy load on a scaffold
    C. use only heavy timber for scaffold construction
    D. do not build high scaffolds

36. A reducing tee has one run opening of 2 inches, the second run opening of 14 inches, and the branch opening of 1 inch.
    This tee would be specified as

    A. 1 x 1 1/2 x 2   B. 1 x 2 x 1 1/2
    C. 2 x 1 1/2 x 1   D. 2 x 1 x 1 1/2

37. A length of pipe is to be fitted with a 90° elbow at each end. The center to center distance between elbows is to be 4'6". The center to end dimension of each elbow is 2" and the thread engagement is 1/2".
    The length to which the pipe should be cut is

    A. 4'1"   B. 4'2"   C. 4'3"   D. 4'4 1/2"

38. Sheet metal seams are sometimes grooved. The MAIN function of the grooving is to

    A. facilitate making a soldered joint
    B. prevent unlocking
    C. improve the appearance of the joint
    D. save sheet metal

39. When fitting new piston rings in a compressor, the piston ring gap is BEST measured by means of a(n)

    A. feeler gage   B. inside caliper
    C. 6" rule   D. depth gage

40. The ampere-hour rating of a battery depends MAINLY on the

    A. number of cells connected in series
    B. casing composition
    C. quantity of electrolyte
    D. number and area of the battery plates

KEY (CORRECT ANSWERS)

1. C	11. A	21. D	31. D
2. B	12. C	22. C	32. C
3. B	13. A	23. B	33. B
4. C	14. B	24. C	34. D
5. D	15. D	25. B	35. A
6. A	16. A	26. A	36. C
7. B	17. C	27. D	37. C
8. C	18. D	28. B	38. B
9. A	19. A	29. A	39. A
10. D	20. B	30. C	40. D

TEST 2

DIRECTIONS: Each question or incomplete statement is followed by several suggested answers or completions. Select the one that BEST answers the question or completes the statement. *PRINT THE LETTER OF THE CORRECT ANSWER IN THE SPACE AT THE RIGHT.*

1. In making a high wooden scaffold, proper splices in 2 x 4 lumber which is to be used vertically would be made by   1.____

   A. lapping each joint with a cleat below
   B. butting the ends and boxing in the joints with 1" boards
   C. butting the ends and nailing a 2 x 4 over the splice
   D. making half-lap joints

2. With respect to soldering, it is LEAST important that   2.____

   A. the soldering copper be clean and well-tinned
   B. a good flux suitable for the metal being soldered be used
   C. the joint to be soldered be well-cleaned
   D. a lot of solder be used

3. When two sheet metal plates are riveted together, a specified minimum distance must be provided from the edge of each plate to the nearest line of rivets in order to prevent   3.____

   A. the rivet heads from working loose
   B. the rivets from being sheared
   C. tearing of the material between the rivets and the edges of the plates
   D. excessive stress on the rivets

4. A hoisting cable is wound on a 14" drum which is rotating at 5 rpm. The load being raised by this cable will move at an APPROXIMATE linear speed, in feet per minute, of   4.____

   A. 13.5   B. 18.3   C. 70   D. 220

5. Spreaders are used in connection with forms for concrete to   5.____

   A. hold the walls of a form the correct distance apart
   B. anchor a form to the ground
   C. make a form watertight
   D. make the cement spread evenly through the form

6. By curing of concrete is meant   6.____

   A. finishing the surface of the concrete
   B. softening stiff concrete by adding water
   C. keeping the concrete wet while setting
   D. the salvaging of frozen concrete

7. If steel weighs 480 lbs. per cubic foot, the weight of an 18" x 18" x 2" steel base plate is _____ lbs.   7.____

   A. 180   B. 216   C. 427   D. 648

8. Standard wrought iron pipe and extra strong wrought iron pipe of the same nominal size differ in

   A. outside diameter
   B. inside diameter
   C. chemical composition
   D. threading

9. Plunbing system stacks are vented to the atmosphere. These stacks will NOT

   A. relieve the back pressure on traps from the sewer side
   B. prevent the siphoning of traps
   C. ventilate the drainage system
   D. prevent the sewer from backing up into the fixtures

10. The MOST likely cause of accidents involving minor injuries is

    A. careless work practices
    B. lack of safety devices
    C. inferior equipment and material
    D. insufficient safety posters

11. In the maintenance of shop equipment, lubrication should be done

    A. periodically
    B. only if necessary
    C. whenever time permits
    D. only during the overhaul period

12. The total number of cubic yards of earth to be removed to nake a trench 3'9" wide, 25'0" long, and 4'3" deep is MOST NEARLY

    A. 53.1   B. 35.4   C. 26.6   D. 11.8

13. A large number of 2 x 4 studs, some 10'5" long and some 6'5 1/2" long, are required for a job.
    To minimize waste, it would be preferable to order lengths of _____ ft.

    A. 16   B. 17   C. 18   D. 19

14. A 6" pipe is connected to a 4" pipe through a reducer. If 100 cubic feet of water is flowing through the 6" pipe per minute, the flow, in cubic feet per minute, through the 4" pipe is

    A. 225   B. 100   C. 66.6   D. 44.4

15. The type of seam generally used in the construction of sheet metal cylinders of small diameters is the _____ seam.

    A. double edged
    B. folded
    C. double hemmed
    D. simple lap

16. Two branch ventilating ducts, one 12 inches square and the other 18 inches square, are to connect to a square main duct.
    In order to maintain the same cross-sectional area, the dimension of the main duct should be _____ inches square.

    A. 14   B. 20   C. 24   D. 28

17. In reference to preparing mortar, it is CORRECT to say that the lime used

    A. may burn the skin
    B. hastens setting
    C. prevents absorption of water by the brick
    D. decreases the amount of water needed

18. The intercooler of a two-stage air compressor is connected to the compressor unit

    A. before the air intake pipe to the first stage
    B. between the second stage and the receiver
    C. between the two stages
    D. after the receiver .

19. In oxyacetylene welding, the hose that is connected to the oxygen cylinder is USUALLY colored

    A. yellow   B. white   C. purple   D. green

20. When bonding new concrete to old concrete, the surface of the old concrete should be

    A. left untouched   B. dry
    C. carefully smoothed   D. chipped and roughened

21. A sack of Portland cement is considered to have a volume, in cubic feet, of

    A. 1/2   B. 3/4   C. 1   D. 14

22. The purpose of a vacuum breaker used with an automatic flush valve is to

    A. limit the flow of water to the fixture
    B. prevent pollution of the water supply
    C. equalize the water pressure
    D. control the water pressure to the fixture

23. Wiping solder for lead pipe USUALLY has a melting range of _____°F.

    A. 150 to 250   B. 251 to 350
    C. 360 to 470   D. 475 to 600

24. A space heater is to be suspended from a structural beam. The heater should be suspended by a hanger

    A. passing through a hole in the web of the beam
    B. passing through a hole in the flange of the beam
    C. welded to the beam
    D. clamped to the beam

25. With respect to babbitted sleeve bearings, oil grooves are

    A. cut only on the top half
    B. cut only on the bottom half
    C. cut on both halves
    D. never necessary

26. When an employee finds it necessary to work near a live third rail, it is BEST to cover the third rail with a

    A. rubber mat
    B. canvas cloth
    C. board
    D. sheet of heavy paper

27. A 10-inch foundation wall is 11 feet long and 15 feet high. If the compressive strength of the wall is 300 pounds per square inch, the MAXIMUM permissible load on this wall is _____ lbs.

    A. 540,000 B. 495,000 C. 396,000 D. 33,000

28. It is INCORRECT to state that

    A. neat cement contains cement and water
    B. salt is used to hasten the setting of concrete
    C. the strength of concrete is affected by the water ratio
    D. a sidewalk should slope toward the street

29. When sharpening a hand saw, the FIRST operation is to file the teeth so that they are of the same height. This is known as

    A. shaping B. setting C. leveling D. jointing

30. The swing of a lathe is the

    A. diameter of the largest piece that can be turned
    B. distance between centers of the head and tail spindles
    C. size of the face plate
    D. radius of the chuck

31. Assume that the lead screw, stud gear, and spindle of a lathe revolve at the same speed. It is required to cut 10 threads per inch when the lead screw has 6 threads per inch. If the stud gear has 48 teeth, the lead screw gear must have _____ teeth.

    A. 48 B. 60 C. 64 D. 80

32. The safety device used on a crane to prevent overtravel is called a(n)

    A. unloader B. governor
    C. limit switch D. overload relay

33. It is INCORRECT to say that

    A. there is a difference between fittings for threaded drainage pipe and fittings for ordinary threaded pipe
    B. a gasoline torch must be fully filled with gasoline
    C. *Red Brass* pipe contains about 85% copper
    D. loose parts in a faucet may cause noisy operation

34. A requisition for lag screws does NOT require stating the

    A. diameter B. quantity
    C. threads per inch D. length

35. In an accident report, the information which may be MOST useful in decreasing the recurrence of similar type accidents is the

    A. extent of injuries sustained
    B. time the accident happened
    C. number of people involved
    D. cause of the accident

36. Carbon tetrachloride is NOT recommended for cleaning purposes because of

    A. the poisonous nature of its fumes
    B. its limited cleaning value
    C. the damaging effects it has on equipment
    D. the difficulty of application

37. The part of the thread directly measured with a thread micrometer is the

    A. thread height   B. major diameter
    C. thread lead   D. pitch diameter

38. The side support for steps or stairs is called a

    A. ledger board   B. runner
    C. stringer   D. riser

39. A sheet metal plate has been cut in the form of a right triangle with sides of 5, 12, and 13 inches.
    The area of this plate, in square inches, is

    A. 30   B. 32 1/2   C. 60   D. 78

40. The BEST first aid for a man who has no external injury but is apparently suffering from internal injury due to an accident is to

    A. take him at once to a doctor's office
    B. make him comfortable and immediately summon a doctor or ambulance
    C. administer a stimulant
    D. start artificial respiration

KEY (CORRECT ANSWERS)

1. B	11. A	21. C	31. D
2. D	12. D	22. B	32. C
3. C	13. C	23. C	33. B
4. B	14. B	24. D	34. C
5. A	15. D	25. A	35. D
6. C	16. B	26. A	36. A
7. A	17. A	27. C	37. D
8. B	18. C	28. B	38. C
9. D	19. D	29. D	39. A
10. A	20. D	30. A	40. B

EXAMINATION SECTION
TEST 1

DIRECTIONS: Each question or incomplete statement is followed by several suggested answers or completions. Select the one that BEST answers the question or completes the statement. *PRINT THE LETTER OF THE CORRECT ANSWER IN THE SPACE AT THE RIGHT.*

1. A maintenance man complains to you that he is getting all the boring jobs to do. You check and find that his complaint has no basis in fact.
The one of the following which is the MOST likely reason why the maintenance man made such a claim is that he

    A. wants to get even with the supervisor
    B. lives in a world of fantasy
    C. believes the injustice to be real
    D. is jealous of other workers

1.____

2. When on preliminary review of a mechanic's written grievance you feel the grievance to be unfounded, the FIRST step you should take is to

    A. show the mechanic where he is wrong
    B. check carefully to find out why the mechanic thinks that way
    C. try to humor the mechanic out of it
    D. tell the mechanic to stop complaining

2.____

3. Assume that you decide to hold a private meeting with one of your mechanics who has a drinking problem that is affecting his work.
At the meeting, the BEST way for you to handle this situation is to

    A. tell the mechanic off and then listen to what he has to say
    B. criticize the mechanic's behavior to get him to *open up* in order to help him correct his problem quickly
    C. try to get the mechanic to recognize his problem and find ways to solve it
    D. limit the discussion to matters concerning only the problem and look for immediate results

3.____

4. The one of the following which is a generally accepted guide in criticizing a subordinate EFFECTIVELY is to

    A. criticize the improper act, not the individual
    B. put the listener on the defensive
    C. make the criticism general instead of specific
    D. correct the personality, not the situation

4.____

5. The one of the following disciplinary methods by which you are MOST likely to be successful in getting a problem employee to improve his behavior is when you

    A. discipline the employee in front of others
    B. consider the matter to be ended after the disciplining
    C. give the exact same discipline no matter how serious the wrongdoing
    D. make an example of the employee

5.____

6. Of the following statements, the one that is MOST applicable to a disciplinary situation is that discipline should be

    A. used after a cooling-off period
    B. identical for all employees
    C. consistent with the violation
    D. based on personal feelings

7. The one of the following approaches that is MOST important for you to take in evaluating a mechanic in order to increase his work productivity is to

    A. first have him evaluate his own performance
    B. meet with him to discuss how he is doing and what is expected on the job
    C. send him a copy of your evaluation of his work performance and give him the opportunity to submit written comments
    D. express in writing your appreciation of his work

8. Assume that you say to one of the mechanics, *Jim, that job you turned out today was top-notch. I didn't think you could do so well with the kind of material you had to work with.*
   This statement BEST describes an example of your

    A. recognition of the man's work
    B. disrespect for the man's feelings
    C. personal favoritism of the man
    D. constructive criticism of the man's work

9. In general, the OUTSTANDING characteristic of employees over 50 years of age is their

    A. resistance   B. endurance
    C. wisdom   D. job stability

10. You should be interested in the morale of your men because morale is MOST often associated with

    A. mechanization   B. automation
    C. production   D. seniority regulations

11. Assume that the maintenance work order system is about to be changed. Your workers would MOST likely show the LEAST resistance to this change if you

    A. downgrade the old maintenance work order system
    B. tell your workers how the change will benefit them
    C. post the notice of the change on the bulletin board
    D. tell the workers how the change will benefit management

12. Of the following, the BEST way to motivate a newly appointed mechanic is to

    A. explain the meaning of each assignment
    B. make the work more physically demanding
    C. test the mechanic's ability
    D. use as much authority as possible

13. The one of the following which is the LEAST important reason for giving employees information concerning policy changes which will affect them is that employees should know   13._____

    A. why the change is being made
    B. who will be affected by the change
    C. when the change will go into effect
    D. how much savings will be made by the change

14. A foreman who knows how to handle his men will MOST likely get them to produce more by treating them   14._____

    A. alike   B. as individuals
    C. on a casual basis   D. as a group

15. Of the following items, the one that a supervisor has the MOST right to expect from his employees is   15._____

    A. liking the job
    B. a fair day's work
    C. equal skill of all mechanics
    D. perfection

16. The one of the following which is the BEST practice for you to follow in handling a dispute between the workers is to   16._____

    A. side with one of the workers so as to end the dispute quickly
    B. pay no attention to the dispute and let the workers settle it themselves
    C. listen to each worker's story of the dispute and then decide how to settle it
    D. discuss the dispute with other workers and then decide how to settle it

17. You are likely to run into an employee morale problem when assigning a dirty job that comes up often.   17._____
    Of the following, the BEST method of assigning this work is to

    A. rotate this assignment
    B. assign it to the fastest worker
    C. assign it by seniority
    D. assign it to the least skilled worker

18. Of the following, the one that is generally regarded as the BEST aid to high work productivity of subordinates is a supervisor's skill in   18._____

    A. record keeping
    B. technical work
    C. setting up rules and regulations
    D. human relations

19. The BEST way to help a mechanic who comes to you for advice on a personal problem is to   19._____

    A. listen to the worker's problem without passing judgment
    B. tell the worker to forget about the problem and to stop letting it interfere with his work
    C. talk about your own personal problems to the worker
    D. mind your own business and leave the worker alone

20. You are in charge of the maintenance shop and have learned that within the next two weeks the maintenance shop will be moved to a new location on the plant grounds, but you have not learned why this move is taking place. Assume that you have decided not to keep this information from your mechanics until the reason is known but to inform them of this matter now.
Of the following, which one is the BEST argument that can be made regarding your decision?

    A. *Acceptable;* because although the reason is not now known, the mechanics will eventually find out about the move
    B. *Unacceptable;* because the mechanics do not know at this time the reason for the move and this will cause anxiety on their part
    C. *Acceptable;* because the mechanics will be affected by the move and they should be told what is happening
    D. *Unacceptable;* because the mechanics' advance knowledge of the move will tend to slow down their work output

20.___

21. Of the following, the FIRST action for a foreman to take in making a decision is to

    A. get all the facts
    B. develop alternate solutions
    C. get opinions of others
    D. know the results in advance

21.___

22. Assume that you have just been promoted to foreman.
Of the following, the BEST practice to follow regarding your previous experience at the mechanic's level is to

    A. continue to fraternize with your old friends
    B. use this experience to better understand those who now work for you
    C. use your old connections to keep top management informed of mechanics' views
    D. forget the mechanics' points of view

22.___

23. You have decided to hold regular group discussions with your subordinates on various aspects of their duties.
Of the following methods you might use to begin such a program, the one which is likely to be MOST productive is to

    A. express your own ideas and persuade the group to accept them
    B. save time and cover more ground by asking questions calling for yes or no answers
    C. propose to the group a general plan of action rather than specific ideas carefully worked out
    D. provide an informal atmosphere for the exchange of ideas

23.___

24. The principle of learning by which a foreman might get the BEST results in training his subordinates is:

    A. Letting the learner discover and correct his own mistakes
    B. Teaching the most technical part of the work first
    C. Teaching all parts of the work during the first training session
    D. Getting the learner to use as many of his five senses as possible

24.___

25. A new mechanic is to be trained to do an involved operation containing several steps of varying difficulty. This mechanic will MOST likely learn the operation more quickly if he is taught

   A. each step in its proper order
   B. the hardest steps first
   C. the easiest steps first
   D. first the steps that do not require tools

25.____

KEY (CORRECT ANSWERS)

1.	C	11.	B
2.	B	12.	A
3.	C	13.	D
4.	A	14.	B
5.	B	15.	B
6.	C	16.	C
7.	B	17.	A
8.	A	18.	D
9.	D	19.	A
10.	C	20.	C

21. A
22. B
23. D
24. D
25. C

TEST 2

DIRECTIONS: Each question or incomplete statement is followed by several suggested answers or completions. Select the one that BEST answers the question or completes the statement. *PRINT THE LETTER OF THE CORRECT ANSWER IN THE SPACE AT THE RIGHT.*

1. The one of the following job situations in which it is better to give a written order than an oral order is when

    A. the job involves many details
    B. you can check the job's progress easily
    C. the job is repetitive in nature
    D. there is an emergency

    1.___

2. Which one of the following serves as the BEST guideline for you to follow for effective written reports?
Keep sentences

    A. short and limit sentences to one thought
    B. short and use as many thoughts as possible
    C. long and limit sentences to one thought
    D. long and use as many thoughts as possible

    2.___

3. Of the following, the BEST reason why a foreman generally should not do the work of an individual mechanic is that

    A. the shop's production figures will not be accurate
    B. a foreman is paid to supervise
    C. the foreman must maintain his authority
    D. the employee may become self-conscious

    3.___

4. One method by which a foreman might prepare written reports to management is to begin with the conclusions, results, or summary and to follow this with the supporting data.
The BEST reason why management may prefer this form of report is because

    A. management lacks the specific training to understand the data
    B. the data completely supports the conclusions
    C. time is saved by getting to the conclusions of the report first
    D. the data contains all the information that is required for making the conclusions

    4.___

5. Forms used for time records and work orders are important to the work of a foreman PRIMARILY because they give him

    A. the knowledge of and familiarity with work operations
    B. the means of control of personnel, material, or job costs
    C. the means for communicating with other workers
    D. a useful method for making filing procedures easier

    5.___

6. The one of the following which is the MOST important factor in determining the number of employees you can effectively supervise is the

   A. type of work to be performed
   B. priority of the work to be performed
   C. salary level of the workers
   D. ratio of permanent employees to temporary employees

7. Of the following, you will be MOST productive in carrying out your supervisory responsibilities if you

   A. are capable of doing the same work as your mechanics
   B. meet with your mechanics frequently
   C. are very friendly with your mechanics
   D. get work done through your mechanics

8. You have been asked to prepare the annual budget for your maintenance shop.
   The one of the following which is the FIRST step you should take in preparing this budget is to determine the

   A. amount of maintenance work which is scheduled for the shop
   B. time it takes for a specific unit of work to be completed
   C. current workload of each employee in the shop
   D. policies and procedures of the shop's operations

9. When determining the amount of work you expect a group of mechanics to perform in a given time, the BEST procedure for you to follow should be to

   A. aim for a higher level of production than that of the most productive worker
   B. stay at the present production level
   C. set general instead of specific goals
   D. let workers participate in the determination whenever possible

10. You have been asked to set next year's performance goals concerning the ratio of jobs completed on schedule to total jobs worked. A review of last year's record shows that the workers completed their jobs on schedule 85% of the time, with the best ones showing an on-time ratio of 92% and the poorest ones showing an on-time ratio of 65%.
    Using these facts in line with generally accepted goal-setting practices, you should set a performance ratio for the next year on the basis of _____ average with a _____ minimum acceptable for any employee.

    A. 85%; 65%   B. 85%; 70%   C. 90%; 65%   D. 90%; 70%

11. It is important for you to be able to identify the critical parts of a large project such as the remodeling of your maintenance shop.
    The one of the following which is the BEST reason why this is important is that it may

    A. help you to set up good communications between you and your workers
    B. give you a better understanding of the purpose of the project
    C. give you control over the time and cost involved in the project
    D. help you to determine who are your most productive workers

12. When doing work planning for your shop, the factor that you should normally consider LAST among the following is knowing your

    A. major objectives
    B. record keeping system
    C. minor objectives
    D. priorities

13. You have the responsibility for ordering all materials for your maintenance shop. A listing of materials needed for the operations of your shop is long overdue. You realize that you are unable to find time to take care of the inventory personally because of a high priority project you have been working on which has been taking all of your time. You do not know when you will be finished with the project.
    The BEST of the following courses of action to take in handling this inventory matter is to

    A. request that you be taken off the project immediately so that you may take care of the inventory
    B. complete your high priority project and then do the inventory yourself
    C. volunteer to work overtime so that you may complete the inventory while continuing with the project
    D. assign the inventory work to a competent subordinate

14. You have the authority and responsibility for seeing that proper records are kept in your shop. Assume that you decide to delegate to a records clerk the responsibility for collecting the time sheets and the authority to make changes on the time sheets to correct the information when necessary.
    Of the following, which one is the BEST argument that can be made regarding your decision?

    A. *Unacceptable*; because you can delegate only your responsibility but none of your authority to the records clerk
    B. *Acceptable*; because you can delegate some of your authority and some of your responsibility to the records clerk
    C. *Unacceptable;* because you can delegate only your authority but none of your responsibility to the records clerk
    D. *Acceptable;* because you can delegate all your responsibility and all your authority to the records clerk

15. You will LEAST likely be able to do an effective job of controlling operating costs if you

    A. eliminate idle time
    B. reduce absenteeism
    C. raise your budget
    D. combine work operations

16. Of the following actions, the one which is LEAST likely to help in carrying out your responsibilities of looking after the interests of your workers is to

    A. crack down on your workers when necessary
    B. let your workers know that you support company policy
    C. prevent the transfers of your workers
    D. back up your workers in a controversy

17. The term *accountability*, as used in management of supervision, means MOST NEARLY

    A. responsibility for results
    B. record keeping
    C. bookkeeping systems
    D. inventory control

18. Assume that you have been unable to convince an employee of the seriousness of his poor attendance record by talking to him.
    The one of the following which is the BEST course of action for you to take is to

    A. keep talking to the employee
    B. recommend that a written warning be given
    C. consider transferring the employee to another work location
    D. recommend that the employee be fired

19. When delegating work to a subordinate foreman, you should NOT

    A. delegate the right to make any decisions
    B. be interested in the results of the work, but in the method of doing the work
    C. delegate any work that you can do better than your subordinate
    D. give up your final responsibility for the work

20. Of the following statements, the BEST reason why proper scheduling of maintenance work is important is that it

    A. eliminates the need for individual job work orders
    B. classifies job skills in accordance with performance
    C. minimizes lost time in performing any maintenance job
    D. determines needed repairs in various locations

21. Of the following factors, the one which is of LEAST importance in determining the number of subordinates that an individual should be assigned to supervise is the

    A. nature of the work being supervised
    B. qualifications of the individual as a supervisor
    C. capabilities of the subordinates
    D. lines of promotion for the subordinates

22. Suppose that a large number of semi-literate residents of this city have been requesting the assistance of your department. You are asked to prepare a form which these applicants will be required to fill out before their requests will be considered.
    In view of these facts, the one of the following factors to which you should give the GREATEST amount of consideration in preparing this form is the

    A. size of the form
    B. sequence of the information asked for on the form
    C. level of difficulty of the language used in the form
    D. number of times which the form will have to be reviewed

23. A budget is a plan whereby a goal is set for future operations. It affords a medium for comparing actual expenditures with planned expenditures.
    The one of the following which is the MOST accurate statement on the basis of this statement is that

    A. the budget serves as an accurate measure of past as well as future expenditures
    B. the budget presents an estimate of expenditures to be made in the future
    C. budget estimates should be based upon past budget requirements
    D. planned expenditures usually fall short of actual expenditures

24. A foreman who is familiar with modern management principles should know that the one of the following requirements of an administrator which is LEAST important is his ability to

   A. coordinate work
   B. plan, organize, and direct the work under his control
   C. cooperate with others
   D. perform the duties of the employees under his jurisdiction

25. The one of the following which should be considered the LEAST important objective of the service rating system is to

   A. rate the employees on the basis of their potential abilities
   B. establish a basis for assigning employees to special types of work
   C. provide a means of recognizing superior work performance
   D. reveal the need for training as well as the effectiveness of a training program

KEY (CORRECT ANSWERS)

1.	A	11.	C
2.	A	12.	B
3.	B	13.	D
4.	C	14.	B
5.	B	15.	C
6.	A	16.	C
7.	D	17.	A
8.	A	18.	B
9.	D	19.	D
10.	D	20.	C

21.	D
22.	C
23.	B
24.	D
25.	A

EXAMINATION SECTION
TEST 1

DIRECTIONS: Each question or incomplete statement is followed by several suggested answers or completions. Select the one that BEST answers the question or completes the statement. *PRINT THE LETTER OF THE CORRECT ANSWER IN THE SPACE AT THE RIGHT.*

1. One of your subordinates, whom you consider to be a troublemaker because of his poor attitude toward his work, has been complaining to other employees about his work and stirring them up to make similar complaints. For you to respond to his actions discreetly and impersonally without any show of emotion or upset is considered to be

    A. *good* practice; you may change his attitudes for the better
    B. *good* practice; he may be so frustrated by your reaction that he will request a transfer
    C. *poor* practice; other employees may follow his example and choose him as their spokesman
    D. *poor* practice; he may not know how to respond to your lack of emotion

2. The practice of a foreman's requesting his subordinates to submit suggestions regarding ways of reducing costs is

    A. *inadvisable;* reducing costs is the foreman's responsibility, not that of his subordinates
    B. *inadvisable* he may waste a great deal of time by having to review worthless suggestions
    C. *advisable;* it will give subordinates something to do when they have no work to occupy them
    D. *advisable;* asking subordinates for ideas on cost reduction will make them feel more involved in the work process

3. Of the following, which is the BEST way to store steel pipe and other similarly shaped metal pieces?

    A. Stack in layers, with alternating rows of materials placed lengthwise and widthwise
    B. Stack in a pyramid shape, with sheets of wood placed between the layers
    C. Stack in layers, with strips of iron, the ends of which are turned up, placed between the layers
    D. In vertical rows, upright against a wall

4. Which one of the following is NOT a usual hazard of handling and servicing storage batteries?

    A. Acid burns   B. Bruised knuckles
    C. Lead poisoning   D. Electric shock

5. As a foreman, at which point should you report an employee to your superior for working in an unsafe manner?

    A. The first time he does something that endangers himself or another employee
    B. Usually not at all; this is a matter that should be handled by the foreman
    C. When you become aware of a pattern of unsafe operations in his work
    D. When an accident occurs

6. In order to prevent a fire, oily work rags should be

   A. kept in covered metal containers
   B. kept in neat piles in a well-ventilated area
   C. kept in open storage boxes, at least ten feet away from any flammable material
   D. wrapped in newspaper and stacked neatly against a fireproof wall

7. For which one of the following uses would it be UNSAFE to use a carpenter's hammer? Striking a

   A. casing nail   B. hand punch
   C. hardened steel surface   D. plastic surface

8. When a certain gasoline tank is filled to capacity, it holds 420 gallons. If it is 3/4 full, the number of gallons of gasoline it is holding is

   A. 280   B. 315   C. 360   D. 375

9. Eight men working full time take 16 days to do a job. How long should it take if four men do this job? _____ days.

   A. 26   B. 28   C. 32   D. 38

10. If 20 feet of lumber costs $62.00, the cost of 45 feet would be

    A. $136.25   B. $139.50   C. $144.25   D. $149.50

11.

Shown above is a rectangle (JKLM) inside another rectangle (NPSR). What is the area of the shaded portion if LM measures 20 feet, JL measures 30 feet, NR measures 45 feet, and RS measures 55 feet?
_____ square feet.

   A. 600   B. 975   C. 1,875   D. 2,475

12. To produce a certain cleaning compound, four materials, W, X, Y, and Z, are combined by mixing 6 pounds of W, 5 pounds of X, 3 pounds of Y, and 1 pound of Z.
    In order to make up 270 pounds of this cleaning compound, the number of pounds of W required is _____ pounds.

    A. 100   B. 108   C. 112   D. 120

13. The normal work week for a laborer is 35 hours.
    If a laborer spends 27 hours at Job Location A and the rest of his work week at Job Location B, the percentage of time spent at Job Location B is MOST NEARLY _____ percent.

    A. 19   B. 21   C. 23   D. 25

14. Which one of the following is the GENERALLY recommended method of assigning work to your subordinates?

    A. Jobs are given to each man according to his ability to perform the job.
    B. Jobs that take the shortest time are given to the workers with the greatest seniority.
    C. The same amount of work is distributed to each man all of the time.
    D. Least important jobs are given to the less experienced workers.

15. Which one of the following tasks USUALLY requires two men to work together until the task is completed?

    A. Removing glass partitions from one location and reinstalling them in another
    B. Repairing a leaking faucet
    C. Filling requisitions from stock bins
    D. Clearing walkways of ice and snow

Questions 16–17.

DIRECTIONS: Questions 16 and 17 are to be answered on the basis of the following report.

To: Al Forbes   Date: March 30
      Director, Building Maintenance
                                              Subject:
From: Jim Harris
      Foreman

On March 30, at 10:30 A.M., while working on a piece of sheet metal in the machine shop, Steve Farrell cut his hand so badly that he was rushed to the hospital and required 10 stitches. After the accident, it was determined that Steve had not been wearing gloves when the accident occurred. It is, therefore, suggested that safety procedures for materials handling be reviewed so that an accident such as this may be prevented in the future.

16. The subject of the report has been left out.
    Which of the following would be BEST as the subject of this report?

    A. Dangerous Conditions in the Machine Shop
    B. Carelessness of Employees Working in the Machine Shop
    C. Procedures for Handling Accidents
    D. Report of Accident Due to Unsafe Materials Handling

17. Of the following, this report is unsatisfactory because it omits 17.____
    A. a recommendation for disciplinary action against Steve Farrell
    B. details regarding how the accident occurred
    C. Steve Farrell's prior accident record
    D. the number of sick days that Steve Farrell has available

18. Suppose an employee under your supervision appears to be developing the habit of 18.____
    wandering off for a half-hour or more almost every afternoon without offering any explanation.
    The FIRST thing you should do in this situation is to

    A. assign extra work to the employee so that he will have no time to wander off
    B. reprimand the employee officially and give him a copy of the reprimand
    C. transfer the employee to another type of work and observe if his behavior remains the same
    D. talk to the employee about the reasons why he is leaving the job site

19. Of the following, the MAIN advantage of having one employee responsible for the issu- 19.____
    ance of tools is

    A. it assures that the right tool will be used for a particular job
    B. tools will be less likely to be damaged
    C. it insures accountability for the tools
    D. it discourages the use of an employee's personal tools

20. After being inspected, a new ladder is usually coated with a preservative such as clear 20.____
    varnish.
    Of the following, the MAIN reason for using a clear preservative is that

    A. the name of the department imprinted on the ladder can be easily identified
    B. defects occurring after the inspection can be easily noticed
    C. workers using the ladder are likely to maintain a new ladder in good condition
    D. cracks in the ladder are less likely to occur than if the ladder were painted

KEY (CORRECT ANSWERS)

1.	A	11.	C
2.	D	12.	B
3.	C	13.	C
4.	C	14.	A
5.	C	15.	A
6.	A	16.	D
7.	C	17.	B
8.	B	18.	D
9.	C	19.	C
10.	B	20.	B

TEST 2

DIRECTIONS: Each question or incomplete statement is followed by several suggested answers or completions. Select the one that BEST answers the question or completes the statement. *PRINT THE LETTER OF THE CORRECT ANSWER IN THE SPACE AT THE RIGHT.*

1. Assume that you, a foreman, expect that some of your workers will have an objection to an order that you must issue.
 If it is not an emergency order, it is MOST advisable for you to

    A. explain to your workers that you do not agree with the order, but that you have no power to do anything but follow it
    B. issue the order without comment and discourage discussion or objections by your workers
    C. state and explain the order carefully to your workers and allow them time to ask questions and to discuss with you their objections
    D. warn your workers before issuing the order that you will take disciplinary action against anyone who resists carrying out the order

    1.____

2. On the job, practical jokes have been played frequently upon one particular man under your supervision. When you, as a foreman, ask the reason for such behavior by the men who play these tricks, they say they do this because the victim invites these tricks upon himself.
 Of the following, it is MOST appropriate for you, the foreman, to FIRST

    A. warn each man involved in such acts that these practical jokes must be discontinued immediately
    B. post a written notice addressed to all the men under your supervision warning them of the dangers involved in playing practical jokes
    C. review the work schedule of your subordinates to see that they have enough work to occupy them for a full day
    D. ask the man on whom the tricks were played if he resents being the victim of such tricks

    2.____

3. Under which one of the following circumstances would it be BEST for a foreman to give orders in the form of commands rather than requests?
 When a foreman

    A. is giving orders to one employee directly rather than to the entire crew
    B. is giving orders that require additional instructions as the work progresses
    C. is giving orders to his entire crew to cope with a critical situation
    D. has been ordered by his supervisor to furnish a skeleton crew for holiday work

    3.____

4. When carrying objects on a two-wheeled handtruck, placing the heavier objects on the bottom of the load is a

    A. *good* practice, because the lighter objects are less likely to be damaged
    B. *poor* practice, because the lighter objects are more likely to fall off
    C. *good* practice, because more weight can be loaded on the truck
    D. *poor* practice, because it will be harder to start the truck in motion

    4.____

5. Of the following, the MAIN advantage in using a Phillips head screw is that

   A. the threads of the Phillips head screw have a deeper bite than standard screw threads
   B. the screwdriver used on this type of screw is more likely to keep its edge than a standard screwdriver
   C. a single screwdriver fits all size screws of this type
   D. the screwdriver used on this type of screw is less likely to slip than a standard screwdriver

6. One of the reasons why a polyester rope is considered to be the BEST general-purpose rope is that it _____ ropes made of other materials.

   A. does not stretch as much as
   B. is available in longer lengths than
   C. does not fray as much as
   D. contains more strands than

7. A daily inspection tour by the foreman would be of GREATEST benefit to him and his subordinates when the subordinates realize that the foreman

   A. is available to answer any questions they might have about the work
   B. is checking up on them to make certain they are not wasting time
   C. is looking for the type of work that will bring his name to the attention of his superiors
   D. will lend a hand to get the daily work accomplished

8. For you to use different methods of discipline for each employee is considered to be

   A. *good* practice; each employee should be disciplined in a manner that is most effective for him
   B. *good* practice; your employees will be afraid to misbehave because they can no longer predict your behavior
   C. *poor* practice, employees may consider these different methods a sign of indecisiveness and lose respect for you
   D. *poor* practice; an employee who believes he is getting the harshest discipline may become hostile and antagonistic

9. As a foreman, you have just informed your crew that you want them to follow a new procedure when signing out for tools from the tool cabinet.
   Of the following, the MOST efficient method for you to adopt to make certain that your crew is reminded of this new procedure is to

   A. take each man aside and tell him you are counting on him to follow the correct procedure
   B. announce to the men that all tools in the cabinet are stamped with a serial number and the agency name
   C. post instructions for the new procedure at the tool cabinet so the men will be sure to see then when requisitioning tools
   D. question the men at their work sites to learn whether they obtained the tools by following the new procedure

10. For you as a foreman to tell an individual employee how much he is expected to do on a job assignment is a

    A. *good* practice, because he will have a goal to try to reach
    B. *bad* practice, because he will be able to determine if you are giving others the same amount of work
    C. *good* practice, because you will be able to give the individual more detailed instructions on how to do the job
    D. *bad* practice, because he will do the minimum amount of work and not be motivated to continue further

11. A laborer who has worked in your agency for five years has just been transferred into your unit.
    In order for you to be able to plan his assignments properly, the FIRST thing you should do is to

    A. ask him what he already knows about the work handled in your unit
    B. plan a training program for him in which all phases of your unit's operations are covered
    C. assign one of your more experienced laborers to train him in the work of your unit
    D. tell him what you want him to do and then interview him

12. After you have assigned a job to one of your workers, he complains to your superior about the job instead of coming to you with his complaint. He recognizes that it is proper to discuss the complaint with you first. However, he points out that in the past other employees under your supervision have successfully bypassed you with their complaints.
    Which of the following approaches generally would be MOST productive in getting your subordinates to turn to you first with their complaints?

    A. Ask your superior how he handled this complaint, so that you can handle it in the same way when the complaint arises again.
    B. Clarify the steps of the complaint procedure with your employees.
    C. Ask your superior to take no action on the employee complaints, but to refer the employee to you, their supervisor.
    D. Tell your employees that if they do not bring the complaints to you first, they cannot take them to your superior.

13. Of the following, the MAIN reason that on-the-job training is widely used is that

    A. the trainee can be producing while he is being trained
    B. the supervisor can assign several trainees to the training at one time
    C. the trainee can progress at his own speed
    D. most supervisors are well-qualified to conduct on-the-job training

14. Of the following, it is BEST for a foreman to begin a new employee's training right after the new employee has

    A. made several errors in performing the first task he has been given to do
    B. had an opportunity to meet all the other employees having his title
    C. reported for work in the unit
    D. shown an interest in learning more about the job he has been doing

15. As a foreman, you have always handwritten accident reports. However, a new accident reporting procedure requests that you use a printed form which asks specific questions and provides blank spaces where the information about the accident can be filled in.
    Of the following, the MOST important advantage of using this printed form is that

    A. the information can be completed by any one of your workers if you are not available
    B. your supervisor can rely on information in a printed form to be more reliable than a completely handwritten report
    C. you can enter as much or as little information on the form as you think necessary
    D. you will be less likely to omit needed information

16. If you replace a blown fuse, and the replaced fuse has burned out shortly thereafter, the FIRST step that should be taken when the replaced fuse has been damaged is that

    A. this second fuse should be replaced by a new fuse of the same type and amperage
    B. this second fuse should be replaced by a new fuse of slightly greater amperage
    C. the circuit should be disconnected while the cause of the burn-out is determined
    D. a check of all other fuses at the electrical connection should be made to determine if they were in working order

17. When you are placing a 12-foot portable ladder with a non-slip base against the side of a building, the distance from the base of the ladder to the base of the side of the building should be MOST NEARLY, according to general safety rules, _____ feet.

    A. 2   B. 3   C. 4   D. 6

18. A foreman must supply sufficient plywood paneling, each panel measuring 4 feet by 8 feet, to erect a three-sided barrier fence 8 feet high in front of a building entrance. This rectangular area will be closed to the public while the building alterations are made. The longer side of the area measures 24 feet, and each of the shorter sides measures 12 feet.
    The MINIMUM number of plywood panels necessary to erect this fence is

    A. 9   B. 12   C. 18   D. 24

19. The proper saw to use to cut wood with the grain is a _____ saw.

    A. hack   B. crosscut   C. back   D. rip

20. One of your men, Tom Jones, has shown up late for work several times in the past two weeks. The quality of his work, however, is good. This morning, Jones comes in late again.
    Of the following, the FIRST action you should take is to

    A. warn Jones that if his lateness continues he will be disciplined
    B. send Jones to the Personnel Officer for disciplinary action
    C. speak to your own supervisor and ask him what to do in this case
    D. ask Jones why he has been arriving late for work so often lately

20.____

KEY (CORRECT ANSWERS)

1. C	11. A
2. A	12. C
3. C	13. A
4. A	14. C
5. D	15. D
6. A	16. C
7. A	17. B
8. A	18. B
9. C	19. D
10. A	20. D

PHILOSOPHY, PRINCIPLES, PRACTICES, AND TECHNICS
OF
SUPERVISION, ADMINISTRATION, MANAGEMENT, AND ORGANIZATION

TABLE OF CONTENTS

	Page
MEANING OF SUPERVISION	1
THE OLD AND THE NEW SUPERVISION	1
THE EIGHT (8) BASIC PRINCIPLES OF THE NEW SUPERVISION	1
I. Principle of Responsibility	1
II. Principle of Authority	2
III. Principle of Self-Growth	2
IV. Principle of Individual Worth	2
V. Principle of Creative Leadership	2
VI. Principle of Success and Failure	2
VII. Principle of Science	3
VIII. Principle of Cooperation	3
WHAT IS ADMINISTRATION?	3
I. Practices Commonly Classed as "Supervisory"	3
II. Practices Commonly Classed as "Administrative"	3
III. Practices Commonly Classed as Both "Supervisory" and "Administrative"	4
RESPONSIBILITIES OF THE SUPERVISOR	4
COMPETENCIES OF THE SUPERVISOR	4
THE PROFESSIONAL SUPERVISOR-EMPLOYEE RELATIONSHIP	4
MINI-TEXT IN SUPERVISION, ADMINISTRATION, MANAGEMENT, AND ORGANIZATION	5
I. Brief Highlights	5
A. Levels of Management	6
B. What the Supervisor Must Learn	6
C. A Definition of Supervision	6
D. Elements of the Team Concept	6
E. Principles of Organization	6
F. The Four Important Parts of Every Job	7
G. Principles of Delegation	7
H. Principles of Effective Communications	7
I. Principles of Work Improvement	7
J. Areas of Job Improvement	7
K. Seven Key Points in Making Improvements	8

	L.	Corrective Techniques for Job Improvement	8
	M.	A Planning Checklist	8
	N.	Five Characteristics of Good Directions	9
	O.	Types of Directions	9
	P.	Controls	9
	Q.	Orienting the New Employee	9
	R.	Checklist for Orienting New Employees	9
	S.	Principles of Learning	10
	T.	Causes of Poor Performance	10
	U.	Four Major Steps in On-the-Job Instructions	10
	V.	Employees Want Five Things	10
	W.	Some Don'ts in Regard to Praise	11
	X.	How to Gain Your Workers' Confidence	11
	Y.	Sources of Employee Problems	11
	Z.	The Supervisor's Key to Discipline	11
	AA.	Five Important Processes of Management	12
	BB.	When the Supervisor Fails to Plan	12
	CC.	Fourteen General Principles of Management	12
	DD.	Change	12
II.	Brief Topical Summaries		13
	A.	Who/What is the Supervisor?	13
	B.	The Sociology of Work	13
	C.	Principles and Practices of Supervision	14
	D.	Dynamic Leadership	14
	E.	Processes for Solving Problems	15
	F.	Training for Results	15
	G.	Health, Safety, and Accident Prevention	16
	H.	Equal Employment Opportunity	16
	I.	Improving Communications	16
	J.	Self-Development	17
	K.	Teaching and Training	17
		1. The Teaching Process	17
		a. Preparation	17
		b. Presentation	18
		c. Summary	18
		d. Application	18
		e. Evaluation	18
		2. Teaching Methods	18
		a. Lecture	18
		b. Discussion	18
		c. Demonstration	19
		d. Performance	19
		e. Which Method to Use	19

PHILOSOPHY, PRINCIPLES, PRACTICES, AND TECHNICS
OF
SUPERVISION, ADMINISTRATION, MANAGEMENT, AND ORGANIZATION

MEANING OF SUPERVISION

The extension of the democratic philosophy has been accompanied by an extension in the scope of supervision. Modern leaders and supervisors no longer think of supervision in the narrow sense of being confined chiefly to visiting employees, supplying materials, or rating the staff. They regard supervision as being intimately related to all the concerned agencies of society, they speak of the supervisor's function in terms of "growth," rather than the "improvement" of employees.

This modern concept of supervision may be defined as follows: Supervision is leadership and the development of leadership within groups which are cooperatively engaged in inspection, research, training, guidance, and evaluation.

THE OLD AND THE NEW SUPERVISION

TRADITIONAL
1. Inspection
2. Focused on the employee
3. Visitation
4. Random and haphazard
5. Imposed and authoritarian
6. One person usually

MODERN
1. Study and analysis
2. Focused on aims, materials, methods, supervisors, employees, environment
3. Demonstrations, intervisitation, workshops, directed reading, bulletins, etc.
4. Definitely organized and planned (scientific)
5. Cooperative and democratic
6. Many persons involved (creative)

THE EIGHT (8) BASIC PRINCIPLES OF THE NEW SUPERVISION

I. Principle of Responsibility
    Authority to act and responsibility for acting must be joined.
    A. If you give responsibility, give authority.
    B. Define employee duties clearly.
    C. Protect employees from criticism by others.
    D. Recognize the rights as well as obligations of employees.
    E. Achieve the aims of a democratic society insofar as it is possible within the area of your work.
    F. Establish a situation favorable to training and learning.
    G. Accept ultimate responsibility for everything done in your section, unit, office, division, department.
    H. Good administration and good supervision are inseparable.

II. Principle of Authority
The success of the supervisor is measured by the extent to which the power of authority is not used.
   A. Exercise simplicity and informality in supervision
   B. Use the simplest machinery of supervision
   C. If it is good for the organization as a whole, it is probably justified.
   D. Seldom be arbitrary or authoritative.
   E. Do not base your work on the power of position or of personality.
   F. Permit and encourage the free expression of opinions.

III. Principle of Self-Growth
The success of the supervisor is measured by the extent to which, and the speed with which, he is no longer needed.
   A. Base criticism on principles, not on specifics.
   B. Point out higher activities to employees.
   C. Train for self-thinking by employees to meet new situations.
   D. Stimulate initiative, self-reliance, and individual responsibility
   E. Concentrate on stimulating the growth of employees rather than on removing defects.

IV. Principle of Individual Worth
Respect for the individual is a paramount consideration in supervision.
   A. Be human and sympathetic in dealing with employees.
   B. Don't nag about things to be done.
   C. Recognize the individual differences among employees and seek opportunities to permit best expression of each personality.

V. Principle of Creative Leadership
The best supervision is that which is not apparent to the employee.
   A. Stimulate, don't drive employees to creative action.
   B. Emphasize doing good things.
   C. Encourage employees to do what they do best.
   D. Do not be too greatly concerned with details of subject or method.
   E. Do not be concerned exclusively with immediate problems and activities.
   F. Reveal higher activities and make them both desired and maximally possible.
   G. Determine procedures in the light of each situation but see that these are derived from a sound basic philosophy.
   H. Aid, inspire, and lead so as to liberate the creative spirit latent in all good employees.

VI. Principle of Success and Failure
There are no unsuccessful employees, only unsuccessful supervisors who have failed to give proper leadership.
   A. Adapt suggestions to the capacities, attitudes, and prejudices of employees.
   B. Be gradual, be progressive, be persistent.
   C. Help the employee find the general principle; have the employee apply his own problem to the general principle.
   D. Give adequate appreciation for good work and honest effort.
   E. Anticipate employee difficulties and help to prevent them.
   F. Encourage employees to do the desirable things they will do anyway.
   G. Judge your supervision by the results it secures.

VII. Principle of Science
Successful supervision is scientific, objective, and experimental. It is based on facts, not on prejudices.
   A. Be cumulative in results.
   B. Never divorce your suggestions from the goals of training.
   C. Don't be impatient of results.
   D. Keep all matters on a professional, not a personal, level.
   E. Do not be concerned exclusively with immediate problems and activities.
   F. Use objective means of determining achievement and rating where possible.

VIII. Principle of Cooperation
Supervision is a cooperative enterprise between supervisor and employee.
   A. Begin with conditions as they are.
   B. Ask opinions of all involved when formulating policies.
   C. Organization is as good as its weakest link.
   D. Let employees help to determine policies and department programs.
   E. Be approachable and accessible—physically and mentally.
   F. Develop pleasant social relationships.

WHAT IS ADMINISTRATION

Administration is concerned with providing the environment, the material facilities, and the operational procedures that will promote the maximum growth and development of supervisors and employees. (Organization is an aspect and a concomitant of administration.)

There is no sharp line of demarcation between supervision and administration; these functions are intimately interrelated and, often, overlapping. They are complementary activities.

I. Practices Commonly Classed as "Supervisory"
   A. Conducting employees' conferences
   B. Visiting sections, units, offices, divisions, departments
   C. Arranging for demonstrations
   D. Examining plans
   E. Suggesting professional reading
   F. Interpreting bulletins
   G. Recommending in-service training courses
   H. Encouraging experimentation
   I. Appraising employee morale
   J. Providing for intervisitation

II. Practices Commonly Classified as "Administrative"
   A. Management of the office
   B. Arrangement of schedules for extra duties
   C. Assignment of rooms or areas
   D. Distribution of supplies
   E. Keeping records and reports
   F. Care of audio-visual materials
   G. Keeping inventory records
   H. Checking record cards and books

I. Programming special activities
J. Checking on the attendance and punctuality of employees

III. Practices Commonly Classified as Both "Supervisory" and "Administrative"
A. Program construction
B. Testing or evaluating outcomes
C. Personnel accounting
D. Ordering instructional materials

RESPONSIBILITIES OF THE SUPERVISOR

A person employed in a supervisory capacity must constantly be able to improve his own efficiency and ability. He represent the employer to the employees and only continuous self-examination can make him a capable supervisor.

Leadership and training are the supervisor's responsibility. An efficient working unit is one in which the employees work with the supervisor. It is his job to bring out the best in his employees. He must always be relaxed, courteous, and calm in his association with his employees. Their feelings are important, and a harsh attitude does not develop the most efficient employees.

COMPETENCES OF THE SUPERVISOR

I. Complete knowledge of the duties and responsibilities of his position.
II. To be able to organize a job, plan ahead, and carry through.
III. To have self-confidence and initiative.
IV. To be able to handle the unexpected situation and make quick decisions.
V. To be able to properly train subordinates in the positions they are best suited for.
VI. To be able to keep good human relations among his subordinates.
VII. To be able to keep good human relations between his subordinates and himself and to earn their respect and trust.

THE PROFESSIONAL SUPERVISOR-EMPLOYEE RELATIONSHIP

There are two kinds of efficiency: one kind is only apparent and is produced in organizations through the exercise of mere discipline; this is but a simulation of the second, or true, efficiency which springs from spontaneous cooperation. If you are a manager, no matter how great or small your responsibility, it is your job, in the final analysis, to create and develop this involuntary cooperation among the people whom you supervise. For, no matter how powerful a combination of money, machines, and materials a company may have, this is a dead and sterile thing without a team of willing, thinking, and articulate people to guide it.

The following 21 points are presented as indicative of the exemplary basic relationship that should exist between supervisor and employee:

1. Each person wants to be liked and respected by his fellow employee and wants to be treated with consideration and respect by his superior.
2. The most competent employee will make an error. However, in a unit where good relations exist between the supervisor and his employees, tenseness and fear do not exist. Thus, errors are not hidden or covered up, and the efficiency of a unit is not impaired.

3. Subordinates resent rules, regulations, or orders that are unreasonable or unexplained.
4. Subordinates are quick to resent unfairness, harshness, injustices, and favoritism.
5. An employee will accept responsibility if he knows that he will be complimented for a job well done, and not too harshly chastised for failure; that his supervisor will check the cause of the failure, and, if it was the supervisor's fault, he will assume the blame therefore. If it was the employee's fault, his supervisor will explain the correct method or means of handling the responsibility.
6. An employee wants to receive credit for a suggestion he has made, that is used. If a suggestion cannot be used, the employee is entitled to an explanation. The supervisor should not say "no" and close the subject.
7. Fear and worry slow up a worker's ability. Poor working environment can impair his physical and mental health. A good supervisor avoids forceful methods, threats, and arguments to get a job done.
8. A forceful supervisor is able to train his employees individually and as a team, and is able to motivate them in the proper channels.
9. A mature supervisor is able to properly evaluate his subordinates and to keep them happy and satisfied.
10. A sensitive supervisor will never patronize his subordinates.
11. A worthy supervisor will respect his employees' confidences.
12. Definite and clear-cut responsibilities should be assigned to each executive.
13. Responsibility should always be coupled with corresponding authority.
14. No change should be made in the scope or responsibilities of a position without a definite understanding to that effect on the part of all persons concerned.
15. No executive or employee, occupying a single position in the organization, should be subject to definite orders from more than one source.
16. Orders should never be given to subordinates over the head of a responsible executive. Rather than do this, the officer in question should be supplanted.
17. Criticisms of subordinates should, whoever possible, be made privately, and in no case should a subordinate be criticized in the presence of executives or employees of equal or lower rank.
18. No dispute or difference between executives or employees as to authority or responsibilities should be considered too trivial for prompt and careful adjudication.
19. Promotions, wage changes, and disciplinary action should always be approved by the executive immediately superior to the one directly responsible.
20. No executive or employee should ever be required, or expected, to be at the same time an assistant to, and critic of, another.
21. Any executive whose work is subject to regular inspection should, wherever practicable, be given the assistance and facilities necessary to enable him to maintain an independent check of the quality of his work.

MINI-TEXT IN SUPERVISION, ADMINISTRATION, MANAGEMENT, AND ORGANIZATION

I. Brief Highlights

Listed concisely and sequentially are major headings and important data in the field for quick recall and review.

A. Levels of Management
Any organization of some size has several levels of management. In terms of a ladder, the levels are:

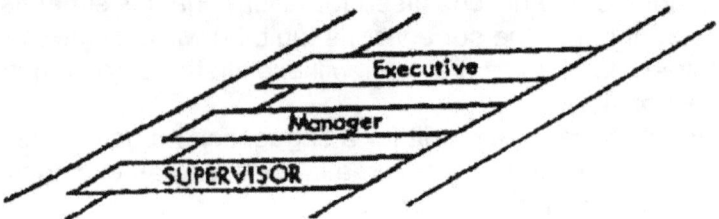

The first level is very important because it is the beginning point of management leadership.

B. What the Supervisor Must Learn
A supervisor must learn to:
1. Deal with people and their differences
2. Get the job done through people
3. Recognize the problems when they exist
4. Overcome obstacles to good performance
5. Evaluate the performance of people
6. Check his own performance in terms of accomplishment

C. A Definition of Supervisor
The term supervisor means any individual having authority, in the interests of the employer, to hire, transfer, suspend, lay-off, recall, promote, discharge, assign, reward, or discipline other employees or responsibility to direct them, or to adjust their grievances, or effectively to recommend such action, if, in connection with the foregoing, exercise of such authority is not of a merely routine or clerical nature but requires the use of independent judgment.

D. Elements of the Team Concept
What is involved in teamwork? The component parts are:
1. Members
2. A leader
3. Goals
4. Plans
5. Cooperation
6. Spirit

E. Principles of Organization
1. A team member must know what his job is.
2. Be sure that the nature and scope of a job are understood.
3. Authority and responsibility should be carefully spelled out.
4. A supervisor should be permitted to make the maximum number of decisions affecting his employees.
5. Employees should report to only one supervisor.
6. A supervisor should direct only as many employees as he can handle effectively.
7. An organization plan should be flexible.

8. Inspection and performance of work should be separate.
   9. Organizational problems should receive immediate attention.
   10. Assign work in line with ability and experience.

F. The Four Important Parts of Every Job
   1. Inherent in every job is the *accountability* for results.
   2. A second set of factors in every job is *responsibilities*.
   3. Along with duties and responsibilities one must have the *authority* to act within certain limits without obtaining permission to proceed.
   4. No job exists in a vacuum. The supervisor is surrounded by key *relationships*.

G. Principles of Delegation
   Where work is delegated for the first time, the supervisor should think in terms of these questions:
   1. Who is best qualified to do this?
   2. Can an employee improve his abilities by doing this?
   3. How long should an employee spend on this?
   4. Are there any special problems for which he will need guidance?
   5. How broad a delegation can I make?

H. Principles of Effective Communications
   1. Determine the media.
   2. To whom directed?
   3. Identification and source authority.
   4. Is communication understood?

I. Principles of Work Improvement
   1. Most people usually do only the work which is assigned to them.
   2. Workers are likely to fit assigned work into the time available to perform it.
   3. A good workload usually stimulates output.
   4. People usually do their best work when they know that results will be reviewed or inspected.
   5. Employees usually feel that someone else is responsible for conditions of work, workplace layout, job methods, type of tools/equipment, and other such factors.
   6. Employees are usually defensive about their job security.
   7. Employees have natural resistance to change.
   8. Employees can support or destroy a supervisor.
   9. A supervisor usually earns the respect of his people through his personal example of diligence and efficiency.

J. Areas of Job Improvement
   The areas of job improvement are quite numerous, but the most common ones which a supervisor can identify and utilize are:
   1. Departmental layout
   2. Flow of work
   3. Workplace layout
   4. Utilization of manpower
   5. Work methods
   6. Materials handling

7. Utilization
8. Motion economy

K. Seven Key Points in Making Improvements
1. Select the job to be improved
2. Study how it is being done now
3. Question the present method
4. Determine actions to be taken
5. Chart proposed method
6. Get approval and apply
7. Solicit worker participation

l. Corrective Techniques of Job Improvement
Specific Problems
1. Size of workload
2. Inability to meet schedules
3. Strain and fatigue
4. Improper use of men and skills
5. Waste, poor quality, unsafe conditions
6. Bottleneck conditions that hinder output
7. Poor utilization of equipment and machine
8. Efficiency and productivity of labor

General Improvement
1. Departmental layout
2. Flow of work
3. Work plan layout
4. Utilization of manpower
5. Work methods
6. Materials handling
7. Utilization of equipment
8. Motion economy

Corrective Techniques
1. Study with scale model
2. Flow chart study
3. Motion analysis
4. Comparison of units produced to standard allowance
5. Methods analysis
6. Flow chart and equipment study
7. Down time vs. running time
8. Motion analysis

M. A Planning Checklist
1. Objectives
2. Controls
3. Delegations
4. Communications
5. Resources
6. Manpower

7. Equipment
8. Supplies and materials
9. Utilization of time
10. Safety
11. Money
12. Work
13. Timing of improvements

N. Five Characteristics of Good Directions
In order to get results, directions must be:
1. Possible of accomplishment
2. Agreeable with worker interests
3. Related to mission
4. Planned and complete
5. Unmistakably clear

O. Types of Directions
1. Demands or direct orders
2. Requests
3. Suggestion or implication
4. volunteering

P. Controls
A typical listing of the overall areas in which the supervisor should establish controls might be:
1. Manpower
2. Materials
3. Quality of work
4. Quantity of work
5. Time
6. Space
7. Money
8. Methods

Q. Orienting the New Employee
1. Prepare for him
2. Welcome the new employee
3. Orientation for the job
4. Follow-up

R. Checklist for Orienting New Employees   Yes   No
1. Do you appreciate the feelings of new employees
   when they first report for work?   ___   ___
2. Are you aware of the fact that the new employee must
   make a big adjustment to his job?   ___   ___
3. Have you given him good reasons for liking the job and
   the organization?   ___   ___
4. Have you prepared for his first day on the job?   ___   ___
5. Did you welcome him cordially and make him feel needed?   ___   ___

	Yes	No

6. Did you establish rapport with him so that he feels free to talk and discuss matters with you? ___ ___
7. Did you explain his job to him and his relationship to you? ___ ___
8. Does he know that his work will be evaluated periodically on a basis that is fair and objective? ___ ___
9. Did you introduce him to his fellow workers in such a way that they are likely to accept him? ___ ___
10. Does he know what employee benefits he will receive? ___ ___
11. Does he understand the importance of being on the job and what to do if he must leave his duty station? ___ ___
12. Has he been impressed with the importance of accident prevention and safe practice? ___ ___
13. Does he generally know his way around the department? ___ ___
14. Is he under the guidance of a sponsor who will teach the right way of doing things? ___ ___
15. Do you plan to follow-up so that he will continue to adjust successfully to his job? ___ ___

S. Principles of Learning
   1. Motivation
   2. Demonstration or explanation
   3. Practice

T. Causes of Poor Performance
   1. Improper training for job
   2. Wrong tools
   3. Inadequate directions
   4. Lack of supervisory follow-up
   5. Poor communications
   6. Lack of standards of performance
   7. Wrong work habits
   8. Low morale
   9. Other

U. Four Major Steps in On-The-Job Instruction
   1. Prepare the worker
   2. Present the operation
   3. Tryout performance
   4. Follow-up

V. Employees Want Five Things
   1. Security
   2. Opportunity
   3. Recognition
   4. Inclusion
   5. Expression

W. Some Don'ts in Regard to Praise
   1. Don't praise a person for something he hasn't done.
   2. Don't praise a person unless you can be sincere.
   3. Don't be sparing in praise just because your superior withholds it from you.
   4. Don't let too much time elapse between good performance and recognition of it

X. How to Gain Your Workers' Confidence
   Methods of developing confidence include such things as:
   1. Knowing the interests, habits, hobbies of employees
   2. Admitting your own inadequacies
   3. Sharing and telling of confidence in others
   4. Supporting people when they are in trouble
   5. Delegating matters that can be well handled
   6. Being frank and straightforward about problems and working conditions
   7. Encouraging others to bring their problems to you
   8. Taking action on problems which impede worker progress

Y. Sources of Employee Problems
   On-the-job causes might be such things as:
   1. A feeling that favoritism is exercised in assignments
   2. Assignment of overtime
   3. An undue amount of supervision
   4. Changing methods or systems
   5. Stealing of ideas or trade secrets
   6. Lack of interest in job
   7. Threat of reduction in force
   8. Ignorance or lack of communications
   9. Poor equipment
   10. Lack of knowing how supervisor feels toward employee
   11. Shift assignments

   Off-the-job problems might have to do with:
   1. Health
   2. Finances
   3. Housing
   4. Family

Z. The Supervisor's Key to Discipline
   There are several key points about discipline which the supervisor should keep in mind:
   1. Job discipline is one of the disciplines of life and is directed by the supervisor.
   2. It is more important to correct an employee fault than to fix blame for it.
   3. Employee performance is affected by problems both on the job and off.
   4. Sudden or abrupt changes in behavior can be indications of important employee problems.
   5. Problems should be dealt with as soon as possible after they are identified.
   6. The attitude of the supervisor may have more to do with solving problems than the techniques of problem solving.
   7. Correction of employee behavior should be resorted to only after the supervisor is sure that training or counseling will not be helpful.

8. Be sure to document your disciplinary actions.
9. Make sure that you are disciplining on the basis of facts rather than personal feelings.
10. Take each disciplinary step in order, being careful not to make snap judgments, or decisions based on impatience.

AA. Five Important Processes of Management
1. Planning
2. Organizing
3. Scheduling
4. Controlling
5. Motivating

BB. When the Supervisor Fails to Plan
1. Supervisor creates impression of not knowing his job
2. May lead to excessive overtime
3. Job runs itself—supervisor lacks control
4. Deadlines and appointments missed
5. Parts of the work go undone
6. Work interrupted by emergencies
7. Sets a bad example
8. Uneven workload creates peaks and valleys
9. Too much time on minor details at expense of more important tasks

CC. Fourteen General Principles of Management
1. Division of work
2. Authority and responsibility
3. Discipline
4. Unity of command
5. Unity of direction
6. Subordination of individual interest to general interest
7. Remuneration of personnel
8. Centralization
9. Scalar chain
10. Order
11. Equity
12. Stability of tenure of personnel
13. Initiative
14. Esprit de corps

DD. Change

Bringing about change is perhaps attempted more often, and yet less well understood, than anything else the supervisor does. How do people generally react to change? (People tend to resist change that is imposed upon them by other individuals or circumstances.

Change is characteristic of every situation. It is a part of every real endeavor where the efforts of people are concerned.

13

1. Why do people resist change?
   People may resist change because of:
   a. Fear of the unknown
   b. Implied criticism
   c. Unpleasant experiences in the past
   d. Fear of loss of status
   e. Threat to the ego
   f. Fear of loss of economic stability

2. How can we best overcome the resistance to change?
   In initiating change, take these steps:
   a. Get ready to sell
   b. Identify sources of help
   c. Anticipate objections
   d. Sell benefits
   e. Listen in depth
   f. Follow up

II. Brief Topical Summaries

   A. Who/What is the Supervisor?
      1. The supervisor is often called the "highest level employee and the lowest level manager."
      2. A supervisor is a member of both management and the work group. He acts as a bridge between the two.
      3. Most problems in supervision are in the area of human relations, or people problems.
      4. Employees expect: Respect, opportunity to learn and to advance, and a sense of belonging, and so forth.
      5. Supervisors are responsible for directing people and organizing work. Planning is of paramount importance.
      6. A position description is a set of duties and responsibilities inherent to a given position.
      7. It is important to keep the position description up-to-date and to provide each employee with his own copy.

   B. The Sociology of Work
      1. People are alike in many ways; however, each individual is unique.
      2. The supervisor is challenged in getting to know employee differences. Acquiring skills in evaluating individuals is an asset.
      3. Maintaining meaningful working relationships in the organization is of great importance.
      4. The supervisor has an obligation to help individuals to develop to their fullest potential.
      5. Job rotation on a planned basis helps to build versatility and to maintain interest and enthusiasm in work groups.
      6. Cross training (job rotation) provides backup skills.

7. The supervisor can help reduce tension by maintaining a sense of humor, providing guidance to employees, and by making reasonable and timely decisions. Employees respond favorably to working under reasonably predictable circumstances.
8. Change is characteristic of all managerial behavior. The supervisor must adjust to changes in procedures, new methods, technological changes, and to a number of new and sometimes challenging situations.
9. To overcome the natural tendency for people to resist change, the supervisor should become more skillful in initiating change.

C. Principles and Practices of Supervision
1. Employees should be required to answer to only one superior.
2. A supervisor can effectively direct only a limited number of employees, depending upon the complexity, variety, and proximity of the jobs involved.
3. The organizational chart presents the organization in graphic form. It reflects lines of authority and responsibility as well as interrelationships of units within the organization.
4. Distribution of work can be improved through an analysis using the "Work Distribution Chart."
5. The "Work Distribution Chart" reflects the division of work within a unit in understandable form.
6. When related tasks are given to an employee, he has a better chance of increasing his skills through training.
7. The individual who is given the responsibility for tasks must also be given the appropriate authority to insure adequate results.
8. The supervisor should delegate repetitive, routine work. Preparation of recurring reports, maintaining leave and attendance records are some examples.
9. Good discipline is essential to good task performance. Discipline is reflected in the actions of employees on the job in the absence of supervision.
10. Disciplinary action may have to be taken when the positive aspects of discipline have failed. Reprimand, warning, and suspension are examples of disciplinary action.
11. If a situation calls for a reprimand, be sure it is deserved and remember it is to be done in private.

D. Dynamic Leadership
1. A style is a personal method or manner of exerting influence.
2. Authoritarian leaders often see themselves as the source of power and authority.
3. The democratic leader often perceives the group as the source of authority and power.
4. Supervisors tend to do better when using the pattern of leadership that is most natural for them.
5. Social scientists suggest that the effective supervisor use the leadership style that best fits the problem or circumstances involved.
6. All four styles—telling, selling, consulting, joining—have their place. Using one does not preclude using the other at another time.

7. The theory X point of view assumes that the average person dislikes work, will avoid it whenever possible, and must be coerced to achieve organizational objectives.
8. The theory Y point of view assumes that the average person considers work to be a natural as play, and, when the individual is committed, he requires little supervision or direction to accomplish desired objectives.
9. The leader's basic assumptions concerning human behavior and human nature affect his actions, decisions, and other managerial practices.
10. Dissatisfaction among employees is often present, but difficult to isolate. The supervisor should seek to weaken dissatisfaction by keeping promises, being sincere and considerate, keeping employees informed, and so forth.
11. Constructive suggestions should be encouraged during the natural progress of the work.

E. Processes for Solving Problems
1. People find their daily tasks more meaningful and satisfying when they can improve them.
2. The causes of problems, or the key factors, are often hidden in the background. Ability to solve problems often involves the ability to isolate them from their backgrounds. There is some substance to the cliché that some persons "can't see the forest for the trees."
3. New procedures are often developed from old ones. Problems should be broken down into manageable parts. New ideas can be adapted from old one.
4. People think differently in problem-solving situations. Using a logical, patterned approach is often useful. One approach found to be useful includes these steps:
    a. Define the problem
    b. Establish objectives
    c. Get the facts
    d. Weigh and decide
    e. Take action
    f. Evaluate action

F. Training for Results
1. Participants respond best when they feel training is important to them.
2. The supervisor has responsibility for the training and development of those who report to him.
3. When training is delegated to others, great care must be exercised to insure the trainer has knowledge, aptitude, and interest for his work as a trainer.
4. Training (learning) of some type goes on continually. The most successful supervisor makes certain the learning contributes in a productive manner to operational goals.
5. New employees are particularly susceptible to training. Older employees facing new job situations require specific training, as well as having need for development and growth opportunities.
6. Training needs require continuous monitoring.
7. The training officer of an agency is a professional with a responsibility to assist supervisors in solving training problems.

8. Many of the self-development steps important to the supervisor's own growth are equally important to the development of peers and subordinates. Knowledge of these is important when the supervisor consults with others on development and growth opportunities.

G. Health, Safety, and Accident Prevention
1. Management-minded supervisors take appropriate measures to assist employees in maintaining health and in assuring safe practices in the work environment.
2. Effective safety training and practices help to avoid injury and accidents.
3. Safety should be a management goal. All infractions of safety which are observed should be corrected without exception.
4. Employees' safety attitude, training and instruction, provision of safe tools and equipment, supervision, and leadership are considered highly important factors which contribute to safety and which can be influenced directly by supervisors.
5. When accidents do occur, they should be investigated promptly for very important reasons, including the fact that information which is gained can be used to prevent accidents in the future.

H. Equal Employment Opportunity
1. The supervisor should endeavor to treat all employees fairly, without regard to religion, race, sex, or national origin.
2. Groups tend to reflect the attitude of the leader. Prejudice can be detected even in very subtle form. Supervisors must strive to create a feeling of mutual respect and confidence in every employee.
3. Complete utilization of all human resources is a national goal. Equitable consideration should be accorded women in the work force, minority-group members, the physically and mentally handicapped, and the older employee. The important question is: "Who can do the job?"
4. Training opportunities, recognition for performance, overtime assignments, promotional opportunities, and all other personnel actions are to be handled on an equitable basis.

I. Improving Communications
1. Communications is achieving understanding between the sender and the receiver of a message. It also means sharing information—the creation of understanding.
2. Communication is basic to all human activity. Words are means of conveying meanings; however, real meanings are in people.
3. There are very practical differences in the effectiveness of one-way, impersonal, and two-way communications. Words spoken face-to-face are better understood. Telephone conversations are effective, but lack the rapport of person-to-person exchanges. The whole person communicates.
4. Cooperation and communication in an organization go hand in hand. When there is a mutual respect between people, spelling out rules and procedures for communicating is unnecessary.
5. There are several barriers to effective communications. These include failure to listen with respect and understanding, lack of skill in feedback, and misinterpreting the meanings of words used by the speaker. It is also common

practice to listen to what we want to hear, and tune out things we do not want to hear.
6. Communication is management's chief problem. The supervisor should accept the challenge to communicate more effectively and to improve interagency and intra-agency communications.
7. The supervisor may often plan for and conduct meetings. The planning phase is critical and may determine the success or the failure of a meeting.
8. Speaking before groups usually requires extra effort. Stage fright may never disappear completely, but it can be controlled.

J. Self-Development
1. Every employee is responsible for his own self-development.
2. Toastmaster and toastmistress clubs offer opportunities to improve skills in oral communications.
3. Planning for one's own self-development is of vital importance. Supervisors know their own strengths and limitations better than anyone else.
4. Many opportunities are open to aid the supervisor in his developmental efforts, including job assignments; training opportunities, both governmental and non-governmental—to include universities and professional conferences and seminars.
5. Programmed instruction offers a means of studying at one's own rate.
6. Where difficulties may arise from a supervisor's being away from his work for training, he may participate in televised home study or correspondence courses to meet his self-development needs.

K. Teaching and Training
1. The Teaching Process
Teaching is encouraging and guiding the learning activities of students toward established goals. In most cases this process consists of five steps: preparation, presentation, summarization, evaluation, and application.

   a. Preparation
   Preparation is two-fold in nature; that of the supervisor and the employee. Preparation by the supervisor is absolutely essential to success. He must know what, when, where, how, and whom he will teach. Some of the factors that should be considered are:
   1) The objectives
   2) The materials needed
   3) The methods to be used
   4) Employee participation
   5) Employee interest
   6) Training aids
   7) Evaluation
   8) Summarization

   Employee preparation consists in preparing the employee to receive the material. Probably the most important single factor in the preparation of the employee is arousing and maintaining his interest. He must know the objectives of the training, why he is there, how the material can be used, and its importance to him.

b. Presentation
In presentation, have a carefully designed plan and follow it. The plan should be accurate and complete, yet flexible enough to meet situations as they arise. The method of presentation will be determined by the particular situation and objectives.

c. Summary
A summary should be made at the end of every training unit and program. In addition, there may be internal summaries depending on the nature of the material being taught. The important thing is that the trainee must always be able to understand how each part of the new material relates to the whole.

d. Application
The supervisor must arrange work so the employee will be given a chance to apply new knowledge or skills while the material is still clear in his mind and interest is high. The trainee does not really know whether he has learned the material until he has been given a chance to apply it. If the material is not applied, it loses most of its value.

e. Evaluation
The purpose of all training is to promote learning. To determine whether the training has been a success or failure, the supervisor must evaluate this learning.
In the broadest sense, evaluation includes all the devices, methods, skills, and techniques used by the supervisor to keep himself and the employees informed as to their progress toward the objectives they are pursuing. The extent to which the employee has mastered the knowledge, skills, and abilities, or changed his attitudes, as determined by the program objectives, is the extent to which instruction has succeeded or failed.
Evaluation should not be confined to the end of the lesson, day, or program but should be used continuously. We shall note later the way this relates to the rest of the teaching process.

2. Teaching Methods
A teaching method is a pattern of identifiable student and instructor activity used in presenting training material.
All supervisors are faced with the problem of deciding which method should be used at a given time.

a. Lecture
The lecture is direct oral presentation of material by the supervisor. The present trend is to place less emphasis on the trainer's activity and more on that of the trainee.

b. Discussion
Teaching by discussion or conference involves using questions and other techniques to arouse interest and focus attention upon certain areas, and by doing so creating a learning situation. This can be one of the most

valuable methods because it gives the employees an opportunity to express their ideas and pool their knowledge.

    c. Demonstration
The demonstration is used to teach how something works or how to do something. It can be used to show a principle or what the results of a series of actions will be. A well-staged demonstration is particularly effective because it shows proper methods of performance in a realistic manner.

    d. Performance
Performance is one of the most fundamental of all learning techniques or teaching methods. The trainee may be able to tell how a specific operation should be performed but he cannot be sure he knows how to perform the operation until he has done so.
As with all methods, there are certain advantages and disadvantages to each method.

    e. Which Method to Use
Moreover, there are other methods and techniques of teaching. It is difficult to use any method without other methods entering into it. In any learning situation, a combination of methods is usually more effective than any one method alone.

Finally, evaluation must be integrated into the other aspects of the teaching-learning process.

It must be used in the motivation of the trainees; it must be used to assist in developing understanding during the training; and it must be related to employee application of the results of training.

This is distinctly the role of the supervisor.

GLOSSARY OF BRIDGE ENGINEERING AND INSPECTION TERMS

	Page
Abutment ...... Aggregate	1
Allowable Unit Stress ...... Arch, Circular	2
Arch, Multi-Centered ...... Backstay	3
Backwall ...... Batter Pile	4
Bay ...... Berm	5
Blanket ...... Bracing	6
Bracing, (cont'd) ...... Brush Curb	7
Buckle ...... Cantilever Beam, Girder, or Truss	8
Cantilever Span ...... Check Analysis	9
Chord ...... Coefficient of Thermal Expansion	10
Cofferdam ...... Coping	11
Corbel ...... Covered Bridge	12
Cracking (reflection) ...... Curves in Plan and Profile	13
Cut ...... Diaphragm	14
Diaphragm Wall ...... Double Movable Bridge	15
Dowel ...... Drip Bead	16
Drip Hole ...... Expansion Dam	17
Expansion Joint ...... Falsework	18
Fascia ...... Fixed Bearing	19
Fixed Bridge ...... Foundation	20
Consolidated Soil Foundation ...... Girder Bridge	21
Girder Span ...... Guide Roller	22
Gusset ...... Hook Belt	23
Howe Truss ...... Joint	24
Keystone ...... Lateral Bracing	25
Lattice ...... Lock Device	26
Locking Mechanism ...... Pontoon Bridge	27
Retractile Draw Bridge ...... Overpass	28
Packing Ring ...... Pedestal Pier	29
Pile Pier or Bent ...... Pin Joint	30
Pin Packing ...... Priming Coat	31
Protection Fence ...... Reinforced Concrete Cantilever Wall	32
Rigid Frame Bridge ...... Rocker and Camshaft	33
Rolled Beams, Rolled Shapes ...... Sag Rod	34
Sash Brace ...... Shafts	35
Shear Lock ...... Skew Angle	36
Skewback ...... Span	37
Spandrel ...... Spreader	38
Springing Line ...... Stress	39
Stress (cont'd) ...... Sump	40
Superelevation ...... Sway Brace	41
Sway Frame ...... Toggle Joint	42
Tolerance ...... Truss	43
Truss Bridge ...... Warren Truss	44
Washer ...... Weep Hole	45
Weld ...... Wing Wall	46
Wing Wall (cont'd) ...... Working Stress	47

GLOSSARY OF BRIDGE ENGINEERING AND INSPECTION TERMS

A

Abutment. A substructure composed of stone, concrete, brick, or timber supporting the end of a single span or the extreme end of a multispan superstructure and, in general, retaining or supporting the approach embankment placed in contact therewith. (See also RETAINING WALLS, WING WALLS.)

The following types are now commonly used:

Cantilever Abutments. An abutment in which the stem or breast wall is fixed rigidly to the footing. The stem, acting as a cantilever beam transmits the horizontal earth pressure to the footing, which maintains stability by virtue of the dead weight of the abutment and of the soil mass resting on the rear portion, or heel, of the footing.

Cellular Abutment. An abutment in which the space between wings, breast wall, approach slab, and footings, instead of containing the approach fill, is hollow. This amounts to an R/C box or boxes comprising the abutment. On some bridges curtain walls are placed between the pier and abutment to simulate a cellular abutment.

Counterforted Abutment. An abutment which develops resistance to bending moment (or horizontal force) in the stem by use of counterforts. This permits the breast wall to be designed as a horizontal beam or slab spanning between counterforts, rather than as a vertical cantilever slab.

Gravity Abutment. A heavy abutment which resists the horizontal earth pressure by its own dead weight.

Integral Abutment. A small abutment cast monolithically with the end diaphragm of the deck. Although such abutments usually encase the ends of the deck beams and are pile supported, spread footings with a combination backwall and end diaphragm may also be used.

L-Abutment. A cantilever abutment with the stem flush with the toe of the footing, forming an L in cross section.

Spill-Thru Abutment. Consists essentially of two or more columns supporting a grade beam spanning the space between them. The approach embankment is retained only in part by the abutment since the embankment's sloped front and side portions extend with their normal slope to envelop the columns. Also called an arched abutment.

Shoulder Abutment. (*Full-Height Abutment.*) A cantilever abutment extending from the grade line of the road below to that of the road overhead. Usually set just off the shoulder.

Semi-Stub Abutment. Cantilever abutment founded part way up the slope, intermediate in size between a shoulder abutment and a stub abutment.

Straight Abutment. (*Trapezoidal or Block.*) An abutment whose stem and wings are in the same plane or whose stem is included within a length of retaining wall. In general, the stem wall is straight but will conform to the alignment of the retaining wall.

Stub Abutment. (*Perched Abutment, Dwarf Abutment.*) An abutment within the topmost portion of the end of an embankment or slope and, therefore, having a relatively small vertical height. While often engaging and supported upon piles driven through the underlying embankment or in-situ material, stubs may also be founded on gravel fill, the embankment, or natural ground itself.

Aggregate. The sand, gravel, broken stone, or combinations thereof with which the cementing material is mixed to form a mortar or concrete. The fine material used to produce mortar for stone and brick masonry and for the mortar component of concrete is commonly termed "fine aggregate" while the coarse material used in concrete only is termed "coarse aggregate."

Allowable Unit Stress. See STRESS.

Anchorage. The complete assemblage of members and parts whether composed of metal, masonry, wood or other material designed to hold in correct position the anchor span of a cantilever bridge, the end of a suspension span cable or a suspension span backstay; the end of a restrained beam, girder or truss span; a retaining wall, bulkhead, or other portion or part of a structure.

Anchor Span. The span which in conjunction with the uplift resisting anchorage device (if any) located at its outermost end, counterbalances and holds in equilibrium the fully cantilevered portion or arm extending in the opposite direction from the major point of support. See CANTILEVER BEAM, GIRDER, OR TRUSS.

Anchor Bolt. A bolt-like piece of metal commonly threaded and fitted with a nut, or a nut and washer at one end only, used to secure in a fixed position upon the substructure the end of a truss or girder, the base of a column, a pedestal, shoe, or other member of a structure. The end intended to engage the masonry may be formed in various ways depending somewhat upon the conditions attending its setting in final position. Among these are the following:

Hooked. Bent either cold or in a heated condition to form a hook-like anchorage. The hooked bolt is commonly built into the masonry preliminary to the placing of the member to be anchored and it may, therefore, be utilized to engage an anchor bar or other device imbedded in the masonry.

Ragged, Barbed or Fanged. Cut with a chisel to produce fin-like projections upon the surface.

Threaded. Shaped with a machine-cut thread. The thread anchorage is commonly supplemented by a nut, or a nut and anchor plate, when the bolt is to be built into the masonry instead of being set in a drilled hole.

Swedged. (*Notched, Hacked.*) Indented and bulged by swedging or nicked transversely and diagonally, or both, by cutting with a chisel.

Angle of Repose. (*Angle of Internal Friction.*) As applied to approach embankments or other earthwork construction: the batter or slope angle with the horizontal at which a given earth material will slide upon itself from a higher to a lower elevation. At all angles less than the angle of repose, the particles of earth are held in equilibrium by the forces of gravity and friction. Relatively slight variations in the quantity of contained moisture produce marked differences in the angle of repose. The inclined surface of a cut or of an embankment either naturally or artificially produced at the angle of repose is commonly described as being at "natural slope."

Anisotropy. The property of some engineering materials, such as wood, exhibiting different strengths in different directions.

Approach Slab. A heavy R/C slab placed on the approach roadway adjacent to and usually resting upon the abutment back wall. The function of the approach slab is to carry wheel loads on the approaches directly to the abutment, preventing the transfer of a horizontal dynamic force through the approach fill to the abutment stem.

Apron. A waterway bed protection consisting of timber, concrete, riprap, paving or other construction placed adjacent to substructure abutments and piers to prevent undermining by scour.

Arch. In general, any structure producing at its supports reactions having both vertical and horizontal components. However, this definition is not intended to include structures of the rigid frame type, although applicable thereto, but instead to apply only to those having throughout their length a curved shape, either actual or approximated.

Specific types of arches adapted to bridge construction derive their names either from the form of curve (or combination of curves assumed for the development of their intradosal surfaces), the support conditions, or their type of construction. The following constitute a portion of the types in use:

Elliptic Arch. One in which the intrados surface is a full half of the surface of an elliptical cylinder. This terminology is sometimes incorrectly applied to a multicentered arch. (An elliptic arch is fitted to stone masonry arches.)

Circular Arch. One in which the intrados surface is a portion of the surface of a right circular cylinder.

Multi-Centered Arch. One in which the intrados surface is outlined by two or more arcs having different radii by intersection tangentially and disposed symmetrically.

Open Spandrel Arch. An arch having spandrel walls with its spandrel unfilled. The arch ring receives its superimposed loads through these walls and, if necessary, through interior spandrel walls, tie or transverse walls, and/or interior columns.

A structure having the spandrel walls replaced by bays or panels with arches, lintel spans, or other constructions supporting the deck construction and these in turn supported by cross walls or columns resting upon the arch ring. See OPEN SPANDREL RIBBED ARCH.

Open Spandrel Ribbed Arch. A structure in which two or more comparatively narrow arch rings function in the place of an arch barrel. The ribs are rigidly secured in position by arch rib struts located at intervals along the length of the ring. The arch rings support a column type open spandrel construction sustaining the floor system and its loads.

Parabolic Arch. One in which the intrados surface is a segment of a symmetrical parabolic surface (suited to concrete arches).

Spandrel Arch. A stone or reinforced concrete arch span having spandrel walls to retain the spandrel fill or to support either entirely or in part the floor system of the structure when the spandrel is not filled.

Segmental Arch. An arch in which the intrados surface is less than half of the surface of a cylinder or cylindroid. Likewise it may take shape wherein any right section will show a parabolic curvature.

Two-Hinged Arch. An arch which is supported by a pinned connection at each support.

Three-Hinged Arch. An arch with end supports pinned and a third hinge (or pin) located somewhere near mid-span making the structure determinate.

Voussoir Arch. A hingeless arch with both supports fixed against rotation. Originally built of wedge-shaped stone blocks or voussoirs, the hingeless arch may also be built of concrete.

Arch Barrel. An arch ring that extends the width of the structure.

Arch Rib. An arch ring unit used in unfilled and open spandrel arch construction in reinforced concrete. Two or more relatively narrow arch ring units or sections support the columns of the bays or panels. The construction may involve a combination of arch ribs with spandrel walls providing an outward appearance akin to that of an unfilled spandrel arch.

One of the arched girders of a plate girder rib arch.

Arm. 1. The portion of a swing bridge or of a retractile draw bridge which forms the span or a portion of the span of the structure. 2. The rear or counterweight leaf of a bascule span. 3. The overhanging (or cantilever) portion of a cantilever bridge which supports the suspended span. 4. In statics, the perpendicular distance between the two parallel equal and opposite forces of a moment.

Armor. A secondary steel member installed to protect a vulnerable part of another member, e.g., steel angles placed over the edges of a joint.

Axle Load. The load borne by one axle of a traffic vehicle, a movable bridge, or other motive equipment or device and transmitted through a wheel or wheels to a supporting structure.

B

Back. See EXTRADOS.

Backfill. Material placed adjacent to an abutment, pier, retaining wall or other structure or part of a structure to fill the unoccupied portion of the foundation excavation.

Soil, usually granular, placed behind and within the abutment and wingwalls.

Backstay. The portion of the main suspension member of a suspension bridge extending between the tower and the anchorage. When this member continues over the towers from anchorage to anchorage, it does not support any portion of the bridge floor system which may be located between the tower and anchorage members of the structure.

A cable or chain attached at the top of a tower and extending to and secured upon the anchorage to resist overturning stresses exerted upon the tower by the suspension span attached to and located between towers.

Backwall. The topmost portion of an abutment above the elevation of the bridge seat, functioning primarily as a retaining wall with a live load surcharge. It may serve also as a support for the extreme end of the bridge deck and the approach slab.

Backwater. The water of a stream retained at an elevation above its normal level through the controlling effect of a condition existing at a downstream location such as a flood, an ice jam or other obstruction.

The increase in the elevation of the water surface above normal produced primarily by the stream width contraction beneath a bridge. The wave-like effect is most pronounced at and immediately upstream from an abutment or pier but extends downstream to a location beyond the body of the substructure part.

Balance Blocks. Blocks of cast iron, stone, concrete or other heavy weight material used to adjust the counterbalance of swing and lift spans.

Balance Wheel. (*Trailing Wheel.*) One of the wheels attached to the superstructure, normally having only a trailing contact upon a circular track surrounding the pivot of a center bearing swing bridge. These wheels maintain the proper balance and lateral stability of the superstructure by preventing excessive rocking or other motion due to wind pressures, shock from operating irregularities, or other causes. When correctly adjusted, a balance wheel will transmit only its own weight to the track and will revolve without load upon its axle.

Balancing Chain. See COUNTERBALANCING CHAIN.

Ballast. Filler material, usually broken stone or masonry, used either to stabilize a structure (as in filling a crib) or to transmit a vertical load to a lower level (as with a railroad track ballast).

Baluster. One of the column-like pieces composing the intermediate portion of a balustrade. Balusters may be varied in cross-sectional shape from round to square. See BALUSTRADE.

Balustrade. A railing composed of brick, stone or reinforced concrete located upon the retaining wall portion of an approach cut, embankment or causeway or at the outermost edge of the roadway or the sidewalk portion of a bridge to serve as a protection to vehicular and/or pedestrian traffic. Its major elements are: (1) plinth, (2) balusters, and (3) capping. However, the web portion may be built without openings instead of balustered or other open construction. See PARAPET.

Base Metal, Structure Metal, Parent Metal. The metal at and closely adjacent to the surface to be incorporated in a welded joint which will be fused, and by coalescence and interdiffusion with the weld will produce a welded joint.

Base Plate. A plate-shaped piece of steel, whether cast, rolled or forged, riveted upon or by other means made an integral part of the base portion of a column, pedestal or other member to transmit and distribute its load either directly or otherwise to the substructure or to another member.

Batten Plate. 1. A plate used to cover the joint formed by two abutting metal plates or shapes but ordinarily not considered as serving to transmit stress from one to the other. 2. A plate used in lieu of lacing to tie together the shapes comprising a built-up member. 3. A term sometimes used as synonymous with Stay Plates to indicate a plate in which the bar latticing or lacing of a bolted, riveted, or welded member terminates.

Batter. The inclination of a surface in relation to a horizontal or a vertical plane or occasionally in relation to an inclined plane. Batter is commonly designated upon bridge detail plans as so many inches to one foot. See RAKE.

Batter Pile. A pile driven in an inclined position to resist forces which act in other than a vertical direction. It may be computed to withstand these forces or, instead, may be used as a subsidiary part or portion of a structure to improve its general rigidity.

When driven and made fast upon the end of a pile bent or a piled pier located in a stream, river, or other waterway, it functions as a cutwater in dividing and deflecting floating ice and debris.

Bay. As applied to a stringer of multibeam structure, the area between adjacent stringers.

Bead. (*Run.*) A narrow continuous deposit of weld metal laid down in a single pass of fused filler metal.

Beam. 1. A simple or compound piece receiving and transmitting transverse or oblique stresses produced by externally applied loads, when supported at its end or at intermediate points and ends. The beam derives its strength from the development of internal bending or flexural stresses. 2. A rolled metal I-shaped or H-shaped piece. 3. An I-shaped piece or member composed of plates and angles or other structural shapes united by bolting, riveting or welding. In general, such pieces or members are described as built-up beams. These terms are applied to and define, in general terms only, variations in shape, size and arrangement of beam type members of reinforced concrete structures.

Reinforced Concrete Beam. Reinforced concrete beam is a construction wherein the tensile stresses, whether resulting from bending, shear, or combinations thereof produced by transverse loading, are by design carried by the metal reinforcement. The concrete takes compression (and some shear) only. It is commonly rectangular or Tee-shaped with its depth dimension greater than its stem width.

Reinforced Concrete T-Beam. Reinforced concrete T-beam derives its name from a similarity of shape to the letter "T," the head or topmost element of the letter consisting of a portion of the deck slab which is constructed integrally with the R/C beam stem.

Bearing Failure. Concerning the usual materials of construction, a crushing under extreme compressive load on an inadequate support; concerning soil, a shear failure in the supporting soil caused by excessively high pressures applied by a footing or pile.

Bearing. (*Fixed.*) A bearing which does not allow longitudinal movement.

Bearing Pad. A thin sheet of material placed between a masonry plate and the masonry bearing surface used to fill any voids due to imperfection of the masonry plate and bearing surface, to seal the interface, and to aid in even distribution of loads at the interface. The bearing pads may be made of alternating layers of red lead and canvas, of sheet lead, or of preformed fabric pads.

Bearing Seat. Top of masonry supporting bridge bearing.

Bearings. (*Live Load, Front Load, Outer.*) Live load bearings are a class of special bearings or supports installed on movable swing and bascule spans. These are engaged when the bridge is in the closed position taking the load off the trunnions and center pivot and preventing the outer end of the lift span from hammering on the rest pier under live load. Front load bearings are live load bearings placed on the support pier of a bascule bridge, and outer bearings are those on swing span and bascule rest piers.

Bed Rock. (*Ledge Rock.*) A natural mass formation of igneous, sedimentary, or metamorphic rock material either outcropping upon the surface, uncovered in a foundation excavation, or underlying an accumulation of unconsolidated earth material.

Bench Mark. A point of known elevation.

Bent. A supporting unit of a trestle or a viaduct type structure made up of two or more column or column-like members connected at their topmost ends by a cap, strut, or other member holding them in their correct positions. This connecting member is commonly designed to distribute the superimposed loads upon the bent, and when combined with a system of diagonal and horizontal bracing attached to the columns, the entire construction functions somewhat like a truss distributing its loads into the foundation.

When piles are used as the column elements, the entire construction is designated a "pile bent" or "piled bent" and, correspondingly, when those elements are framed, the assemblage is termed a "frame bent."

Berm. (*Berme.*) The line, whether straight or curved, which defines the location where the top surface of an approach embankment or causeway is intersected by the surface of the side slope. This term is synonymous with "Roadway Berm."

A horizontal bench located at the toe of slope of an approach cut, embankment or causeway to strengthen and secure its underlaying material against sliding or other displacement into an adjacent ditch, borrow pit, or other artificial or natural lower lying area.

Blanket. A protection against stream scour placed adjacent to abutments and piers and covering the stream bed for a distance from these structures considered adequate for the stream flow and stream bed conditions. The stream bed covering commonly consists of a deposit of stones of varying sizes which, in combination, will resist the scour forces. A second type consists of a timber framework so constructed that it can be ballasted and protected from displacement by being loaded with stones or with pieces of wrecked concrete structures or other adaptable ballasting material.

Boster. A block-like member composed of wood, metal, or concrete used to support a bearing on top of a pier cap or abutment bridge seat. It may adjust bearing heights and avoid constructing the bridge seat to the crown of the roadway, provide an area that may be ground to a precise elevation, or raise a bearing above moisture and debris that may collect on the bridge seat. See also BRIDGE PAD and BRIDGE SEAT PEDESTAL.

Bolted Joint. See RIVETED JOINT.

Bond. 1. In reinforced concrete, the grip of the concrete on the reinforcing bars, thereby preventing slippage of the bars. 2. The mechanical bond resulting from irregularities of surface produced in the manufacturing operations is an important factor in the strength of a reinforced concrete member. For plain round bar reinforcement, it is the difference between the force required to produce initial slip and the ultimate, producing failure. "Deformed" bars utilize this mechanical bond in conjunction with the surface bond. 3. The mechanical force developed between two concrete masses when one is cast against the already hardened surface of the other.

Bond Stress. A term commonly applied in reinforced concrete construction to the stress developed by the force tending to produce movement or slippage at the interface between the concrete and the metal reinforcement bars or other shapes.

Bowstring Truss. A general term applied to a truss of any type having a polygonal arrangement of its top chord members conforming to or nearly conforming to the arrangement required for a parabolic truss.

A truss having a top chord conforming to the arc of a circle or an ellipse. See PARABOLIC TRUSS.

Box Beam. A rectangular-shaped precast, and usually prestressed, concrete beam. These beams may be placed side by side, connected laterally, and used to form a bridge deck, with or without a cast-in-place slab or topping. In such cases, the beam units act together similar to a slab. Where a C-I-P slab is used and the units are spread, they act as beams.

Box Girder (concrete). A large concrete box-shaped beam, either reinforced or prestressed, usually multi-celled with several interior webs. The bottom slab of the girder serves as a flange only, while the top slab is both a flange and a transverse deck slab.

Box Girder (steel). A steel beam or girder, with a rectangular or trapezoidal cross section, composed of plates and angles or other structural shapes united by bolting, riveting, or welding, and having no interior construction except stiffeners, diaphragms, or other secondary bracing parts.

Recently, large steel multi-cell boxes with interior webs have been used as have composite steel box girders in which the concrete slab forms the top side of the box.

Bracing. A system of tension or of compression members, or a combination of these, forming with the part or parts to be supported or strengthened a truss or frame. It transfers wind, dynamic, impact, and vibratory stresses to the substructure and gives rigidity throughout the complete assemblage. In general, the bracing of a girder or of a truss span employs:

(1) A system of horizontal bracing in the planes of the top and bottom flanges or chords, designated according to its location, the top flange, top chord, top or overhead lateral brac-

ing, and the bottom flange, bottom chord or lower lateral bracing.

(2) Cross or X-bracing when placed transversely in vertical planes between beams and stringers and having diagonal members crossed, sometimes termed "Cross Frame." It functions as a diaphragm.

(3) Sway or buck bracing when placed transversely in vertical or nearly vertical planes between trusses. The term "overhead bracing," when applied here, is more appropriate than when applied to the top chord lateral bracing.

(4) Portal bracing consisting of a system of struts, ties and braces placed in the plane of the end posts of the trusses. Portal bracing may be in the plane of one flange of the end posts and described as a "single plane" portal or it may engage both flanges and be described as a "box portal." Without regard to its shape or details the entire portal bracing member is frequently designated as a "portal."

In general, the bracing of trestle and viaduct bents and towers employs:

(1) Transverse bracing engaging the columns of bents and towers in planes located either perpendicular or slightly inclined and transversely to the bridge alignment.

(2) Longitudinal bracing engaging the columns of bents and towers in planes located either perpendicular or slightly inclined and lengthwise with the bridge alignment.

(3) Horizontal bracing engaging the strut members of the transverse and longitudinal bracing of towers. Commonly this bracing is located in a horizontal position and is supported against sagging by vertical hangers or ties.

Bracket. A projecting support or brace-like construction fixed upon two intersecting members to function: (1) as a means of transferring reactions or shear stress from one to the other, or (2) to strengthen and render more rigid a joint connection of the members, or (3) to simply hold one member in a fixed position with relation to the other.

Breast Wall. (*Face Wall, Stem.*) The portion of an abutment between the wings and beneath the bridge seat. The breast wall supports the superstructure loads, and retains the approach fill.

Brick Veneer. See STONE FACING.

Bridge. A structure providing a means of transit for pedestrians and/or vehicles above the land and/or water surface of a valley, arroyo, gorge, river, stream, lake, canal, tidal inlet, gut or strait; above a road, highway, railway or other obstruction, whether natural or artificial.

In general, the essential parts of a bridge are: (1) the substructure consisting of its abutments and pier or piers supporting the superstructure, (2) the superstructure slab, girder, truss, arch or other span or spans supporting the roadway loads and transferring them to the substructure, and (3) the roadway and its incidental parts functioning to receive and transmit traffic loads.

Bridge (composite). A bridge whose concrete deck acts structurally with longitudinal main carrying members.

Bridge (indeterminate). A structure in which forces in the members cannot be determined by static equations alone.

Bridge (prestressed). A bridge whose main carrying members are made of prestressed concrete.

Bridge Pad. The raised, levelled area upon which the pedestal, shoe, sole, plate or other corresponding element of the superstructure takes bearing by contact. Also called Bridge Seat Bearing Area.

Bridge Seat. The top surface of an abutment or pier upon which the superstructure span is placed and supported. For an abutment it is the surface forming the support for the superstructure and from which the backwall rises. For a pier it is the entire top surface.

Bridge Site. The selected position or location of a bridge.

Bridging. A carpentry term applied to the cross-bracing, nailed or otherwise, fastened between wooden floor stringers, usually at the one-third span points, to increase the rigidity of the floor construction and to distribute more uniformly the live load and minimize the effects of impact and vibration.

Brush Curb. A narrow curb, 9 inches or less in width, which prevents a vehicle from brushing against the railing or parapet.

Buckle. To fail by an inelastic change in alignment (usually as a result of compression).

Buffer. (*Bumper.*) A mechanism designed to absorb the concussion or impact of a moving superstructure or other moving part when it swings, rises or falls to its limiting position of motion.

Built-Up Column. (*Built-Up Girder.*) A column, beam or girder, as the case may be, composed of plates and angles or other structural shapes united by bolting, riveting or welding to render the entire assemblage a unit. A built-up girder is commonly described as a plate girder.

Bulkhead. 1. A retaining wall-like structure commonly composed of driven piles supporting a wall or a barrier of wooden timbers or reinforced concrete members functioning as a constraining structure resisting the thrust of earth or of other material bearing against the assemblage. 2. A retaining wall-like structure composed of timber, steel, or reinforced concrete members commonly assembled to form a barrier held in a vertical or an inclined position by members interlocking therewith and extending into the restrained material to obtain the anchorage necessary to prevent both sliding and overturning of the entire assemblage.

Bumper. See BUFFER.

Buttress. A bracket-like wall, of full or partial height, projecting from another wall. The buttress strengthens and stiffens the wall against overturning forces applied to the opposite face by virtue of its depth in the direction of the loads. A buttress may be either integral with or independent of, but must be in contact with, the wall it is designed to reinforce. All parts of a buttress act in compression.

Buttressed Wall. See RETAINING WALL.

Butt Weld. A weld joining two abutting surfaces by depositing weld metal within an intervening space. This weld serves to unite the abutting surfaces of the elements of a member or to join members or their elements abutting upon or against each other.

C

Cable. One of the main suspension members of a suspension type bridge. Its function is to receive the bridge floor loads and transmit them to the towers and anchorages. See SUSPENSION BRIDGE.

Cable Band. The attachment device serving to fix a floor suspender upon the cable of a suspension bridge. In general this device consists of a steel casting provided with bolts or other appliances to securely seize it upon the cable and prevent the bank from slipping from its correct location.

Camber. The slightly arched form or convex curvature, provided in a single span or in a multiple span structure, to compensate for dead load deflection and to secure a more substantial and aesthetic appearance than is obtained when uniformly straight lines are produced. In general, a structure built with perfectly straight lines appears slightly sagged. This optical illusion is unsatisfactory and is most manifest in relatively long structures over rivers or other water areas.

The superelevation given to the extreme ends of a swing span during erection to diminish the deflection or "droop" of the arms when in open position-cantilevered from the center bearing. The decreased deformation below the normal position reduces the energy required to raise the ends in the closed position to permit the arms to function as simple spans.

Cantilever. A projecting beam, truss, or slab supported at one end only.

Cantilever Abutment. See ABUTMENT.

Cantilever Bridge. A general term applying to a bridge having a superstructure of the cantilever type.

Cantilever Beam, Girder, or Truss. A girder or truss having its members or parts so arranged that one or both of its end portions extend beyond the point or points of support. In general, it may have the following forms: (1) two projecting ends counterbalanced over a center support; (2) a projecting end counterbalanced in part by a portion extending beyond the point of support in the opposite direction, and having at its end an uplift resisting anchorage to complete the condition of equilibrium or, instead, the counterbalancing portion or anchor arm may in itself be adequate to counteract the projecting portion; (3) two projecting ends with an intermediate suspended portion, whose weight is completely counterbalanced by the anchor spans and/or anchorages. The end portions may or may not be alike in design.

Cantilever Span. A superstructure span of a cantilever bridge composed of two cantilever arms or of a suspended span connected with one or two cantilever arms.

Cap. (*Cap Beam, Cap Piece.*) The topmost piece or member of a viaduct, trestle, or frame bent serving to distribute the loads upon the columns and to hold them in their proper relative positions.

The topmost piece or member of a pile bent in a viaduct or trestle serving to distribute the loads upon the piles and to hold them in their proper relative positions. See PIER CAP and PILE CAP.

Capillary Action. The process by which water is drawn from a wet area to a dry area through the pores of a material.

Capstone. 1. The topmost stone of a masonry pillar, column or other structure requiring the use of a single capping element. 2. One of the stones used in the construction of a stone parapet to make up its topmost or "weather" course. Commonly this course projects on both the inside and outside beyond the general surface of the courses below it.

Carnegie Beam. See WIDE FLANGE.

Catch Basin. A receptacle, commonly box-shaped and fitted with a grilled inlet and a pipe outlet drain designed to collect the rain water and floating debris from the roadway surface and retain the solid material so that it may be removed at intervals. Catch basins are usually installed beneath the bridge floor or within the approach roadway with the grilled inlet adjacent to the roadway curb.

Catchment Area. See DRAINAGE AREA.

Catwalk. A narrow walkway for access to some part of a structure.

Cement Paste. The plastic combination of cement and water that supplies the cementing action in concrete.

Cement Matrix. The binding medium in a mortar or concrete produced by the hardening of the cement content of the mortar, concrete mixture of inert aggregates, or hydraulic cement and water.

Center Bearing. The complete assemblage of pedestal castings, pivot, discs, etc., functioning to support the entire dead load of a swing span when the end lifts are released or the span is revolving to "open" or to "closed position."

Center Discs. The assemblage of bronze, steel or other metal discs enclosed in the pivot of a center bearing swing span to reduce the frictional resistance in the operation of the span.

Center Lock. A locking device that transmits shear at the centerline of a double leaf bascule or double swing span bridge. This eliminates deflection and vibration at the center of the span.

Center Wedges. On a swing bridge, the assembly of pedestals and wedges located upon the pivot pier beneath the loading girder and operated mechanically to receive the pivot pier live loads and transmit them direct to the substructure, thus relieving the pivot casting from all, or nearly all, live load stress.

Centering. The supporting structure upon which the arch ring is constructed. This commonly consists of timber or metal framework having its topmost portion shaped to conform with the arch intrados and finished by covering with lagging or with bolsters, the latter being spaced to permit treatment of the mortared joints of stone masonry.

Support for formwork for any slab, beam, or other generally horizontal concrete structure.

Centering Device. The mechanical arrangement or device which guides the span of a bascule or a vertical lift span to its correct location upon its supports when being moved from open to closed position.

Channel Profile. Longitudinal section of a channel.

Chase. A channel, groove or elongated recess built into a structure surface for 1) the reception of a part forming a joint or (2) the installation of a member or part of the structure.

Check Analysis. See LADLE ANALYSIS.

Chord. In a truss, the upper and the lower longitudinal members, extending the full length and carrying the tensile and compressive forces which form the internal resisting moment, are termed chords. The upper portion is designated the upper, or top, chord and correspondingly the lower portion is designated the lower, or bottom, chord. The chords may be paralleled, or the upper one may be polygonal or curved (arched) and the lower one horizontal, or both may be polygonal. In general, the panel points of polygonal top chords are designed to follow the arc of a parabola and are, therefore, truly parabolic chords. Polygonal shaped chords are commonly described as "broken chords."

Chord Members. Trusses are commonly divided lengthwise into panels, the length of each being termed a panel length. The corresponding members of the chords are described as upper, or top, chord members and lower, or bottom, chord members.

Clearance. The unobstructed space provided: (1) in a through or half-through truss or a through plate girder type bridge, and (2) upon a deck truss or girder type bridge for the free passage of vehicular and pedestrian traffic. Clearance is measured in vertical and horizontal (lateral) dimensions and may or may not be determined or regulated by standard (clearance diagram) requirements. Vertical clearance for vehicles is measured above the elevation of the floor surface at its crown dimension while horizontal clearance is commonly measured from or with reference to the edge of travelway.

The unobstructed space provided below a bridge superstructure for (1) the passage of a river or stream with its surface burden of floating debris; (2) the passage of navigation craft commonly designated "clear headway" and (3) the passage of vehicular and pedestrian traffic. This form of clearance is frequently designated "under-clearance" to differentiate it from the provision for the requirements of the transportation service supported by the structure.

The space allowed for (1) the tolerance permitted in the dimensions of structural shapes; (2) the free assembling and adjustment of the elements of members or the members of a structure; and (3) the variations in dimensions incident to workmanship, temperature changes and minor irregularities. Among shop and field workers this condition is sometimes described as "the go and come" or "the play" allowance.

Clear Headway. (*Headway.*) The vertical clearance beneath a bridge structure available for the use of navigation. See CLEARANCE. In tidal waters headway is measured above mean high tide elevation.

Clear Span. The unobstructed space or distance between the substructure elements measured, by common practice, between faces of abutments and/or piers. However, when a structure is located upon a stream, river, tidal inlet or other waterway used by navigation, the clear span dimension is measured at mean low water elevation and may be the distance between guard or fender piers, dolphins or other constructions for the protection of navigation.

Clevis. A forked device used to connect the end of a rod upon a gusset plate or other structural part by means of a pin. It commonly consists of a forging having a forked end arranged to form two eyes or eyelets for engaging a pin and a nut-like portion, constructed integrally therewith, for engaging the correspondingly threaded end of a rod. However, the forked end (clevis) may form an integral portion of a rod without provision for adjustment of its length. An adjustable member having a fixed clevis at one end may be fitted with a thread and nut at its opposite end while one having fixed clevises at its ends may be fitted with either a sleeve nut or a turnbuckle in its midlength portion. Lateral bracing and tie-rod diagonals on old steel trusses often use clevises.

Clevis Bar. A member consisting of a rod having upset threaded ends fitted with clevises for engaging end connection pins. To render a clevis bar adjustable after assembling in a structure its ends are right and left threaded, or it may be constructed with a sleeve nut or a turnbuckle within its length, the end threads upon each of its sections being right and left hand and its clevises forged integrally with the body sections of the bar.

Clip Angle. See CONNECTION ANGLE.

Coefficient of Thermal Expansion. The unit strain produced in a material by a change of one degree in temperature.

Cofferdam. In general, an open box-like structure constructed to surround the area to be occupied by an abutment, pier, retaining wall or other structure and permit unwatering of the enclosure so that the excavation for the preparation of a foundation and the abutment, pier, or other construction may be effected in the open air. In its simplest form, the dam consists of interlocking steel sheet piles. See SHEET PILE COFFERDAM.

Collision Strut. A redundant member intended to reinforce the inclined end post of a through truss against damage from vehicular traffic. It joins the end post at a height above the roadway conceived to be the location of collision contact and, commonly, connects it with the first interior bottom chord panel point. The use of collision struts in highway bridges is limited.

Cold Work. The forming, such as rolling or bending, of a material at ordinary room temperature. Also applied to such deformation of steel elements in service under concentrated forces.

Column. A general term applying to a member resisting compressive stresses and having, in general, a considerable length in comparison with its transverse dimensions. This term is sometimes used synonymously for "post."

A member loaded primarily in compression. See also STRUT, POST, PILLAR.

Composite Joint. A joint in which the strength, rigidity or other requisites of its function are developed by combined mechanical devices, or by a fusion weld in conjunction with one or more mechanical means or appliances. The uncertain functioning of joints of this type makes their use undesirable.

Compound Roller. A roller consisting of a large solid cylinder at the center surrounded by a nest of smaller solid rollers having circular spacing bars engaging their ends and enveloped in a large hollow cylinder which forms the exterior surface of the assemblage. The large roller is commonly bored throughout its length at its center to permit observation of its interior material.

Compression (inelastic). Compression beyond the yield point.

Concrete. A composite material consisting essentially of a binding medium within which are embedded particles or fragments of a relatively inert mineral filler. In portland cement concrete, the binder or matrix, either in the plastic or the hardened state, is a combination of portland cement and water. The filler material, called aggregate, is generally graded in size from fine sand to pebbles or stones which may, in some concrete, be several inches in diameter.

Concrete is used in conjunction with stone fragments or boulders, of "one man" size or larger, imbedded therein to produce "cyclopean" or "rubble" concrete.

Connection Angle. (*Clip Angle.*) A piece or pieces of angle serving to connect two elements of a member or two members of a structure.

Consolidation. The time-dependent change in volume of a soil mass under compressive load caused by pore-water slowly escaping from the pores or voids of the soil. The soil skeleton is unable to support the load by itself and changes structure, reducing its volume and usually producing vertical settlements.

Continuous Girder. A general term applied to a beam or girder constructed continuously over one or more intermediate supports.

Continuous Spans. A beam, girder, or truss type superstructure designed to extend continuously over one or more intermediate supports.

Continuous Truss. A truss having its chord and web members arranged to continue uninterruptedly over one or more intermediate points of support, i.e., having three or more points of support.

Continuous Weld. A weld extending throughout the entire length of a joint.

Coping. A course of stone laid with a projection beyond the general surface of the masonry below it and forming the topmost portion of a retaining wall, pier, abutment, wingwall, etc. In general, the top surface is battered (washed) to prevent accumulation of rain or other moisture thereon.

A course of stone capping the curved or V-shaped extremity of a pier, providing a transition to the pier head proper. When so used it is commonly termed the "starling coping," "nose coping," the "cut-water coping" or the "pier extension coping."

In concrete construction the above terms are used without change.

Corbel. A piece or part constructed to project from the surface of a wall, column or other portion of a structure to serve as a support for a brace, short, beam or other member.

A projecting course or portion of masonry serving: (1) as a support for a superimposed member or members of a structure, or (2) as a part of the architectural treatment of a structure. In stone and brick masonry construction, this form of corbel is termed a "corbel course" implying greater length than that of a simple corbel.

Corrosion. The general disintegration and wasting of surface metal or other material through oxidation, decomposition, temperature, and other natural agencies.

Corrosion (electrolytic). Corrosion resulting from galvanic action.

Cotter Bolt. A bolt having a head at one end and near the opposite end a round hole or a hexagonal slot fitted with a cotter pin in the former or a tapered wedge in the latter. A cotter pin is usually formed by bending a piece of half-round rod to form a loop eye and a split body permitting its end to be splayed, thus holding it in position while a cotter wedge may be split for the same purpose, but either of these locking devices may be undivided and only bent sharply to prevent withdrawal. Cotter bolts are commonly fitted with one or two washers.

A cotter bolt fitted with a key is sometimes termed a "key bolt."

Counter. A truss web member which functions only when the span is partially loaded and shear stresses are opposite in sign to the normal conditions. The dead load of the truss does not stress the counter. See WEB MEMBERS.

Counterbalancing Chain. (*Balancing Chain.*) The chains made a part of the operating equipment of a vertical lift bridge to function as a weight counteracting the varying weight of the supporting cables incidental to the movements of the span.

Counterfort. A bracket-like wall projecting from another wall to which it adds stability by being integrally built with or otherwise securely attached to the side to which external forces are applied tending to overturn it. A counterfort, as opposed to a buttress, acts entirely to resist tensile and bending stresses. It may extend from the base either part or all the way to the top of the wall it is designed to reinforce.

Counterforted Wall. See RETAINING WALL.

Counterweight. A weight placed in position so as to counter balance the weight of a movable part (such as bascule leaf or vertical lift span).

Counterweight Well. (*Tail Pit.*) The enclosed space located beneath the bridge floor at the approach end to accommodate the counterweight and its supporting frame during the opening-closing cycle of the movable span of certain types of bascule bridge structures.

Course. In stone masonry, a layer of stone composed of either cut or uncut pieces laid with horizontal or slightly longitudinally inclined joints.

In brick masonry, a layer of bricks bedded in mortar.

Cover. In reinforced concrete, the clear thickness of concrete between a reinforcing bar and the surface of the concrete.

Cover Plate. A plate used in conjunction with flange angles or other structural shapes to provide additional flange section upon a girder, column, strut or similar member.

Covered Bridge. An indefinite term applied to a wooden bridge having in its construction a truss of any type adaptable to its location requirements. To prevent or delay deterioration of the timbers through infiltration of moisture into the framed or other joints, the entire structure, or instead, only its trusses are covered by a housing consisting of boards and shingles or other covering materials, fastened upon the side girts, rafters, purlins, or other parts intended to receive them. A covered bridge may be either a through or a deck structure. The former may be constructed with pony trusses.

Cracking (reflection). Visible cracks in an overlay indicating cracks in the concrete underneath.

Creep. An inelastic deformation that increases with time while the stress is constant.

Crib. A structure consisting of a foundation grillage combined with a superimposed framework providing compartments or coffers which are filled with gravel, stones, concrete or other material satisfactory for supporting the masonry or other structure to be placed thereon. The exterior portion may be planked or sheetpiled to protect the crib against damage by erosion or floating debris.

A structure consisting of a series of box-like compartments built of round or squared timbers having the crosstimbers (compartment division and end wall timbers) drift bolted and dove-tail framed or half framed to interlock with the side timbers, thus producing a rigid framework of the height desired. A portion of the compartment is constructed with floors to serve as ballast boxes for loading and sinking the crib in its final position after which the remaining compartments are filled or partially filled with gravel, stones or other material to render the entire structure stable against the forces to which it may be subjected.

This latter type of crib is used as a protection against wave action and stream currents producing scour and erosion adjacent to bridge structures to prevent undermining of abutments and piers or other substructure elements and also to serve as a training wall averting changes in shore and bank locations.

Cribbing. A construction consisting of wooden, metal or reinforced concrete units so assembled as to form an open cellular-like structure for supporting a superimposed load or for resisting horizontal or overturning forces acting against it.

Cross Frames. Transverse bracings between two main longitudinal members. See DIAPHRAGM and BRACING.

Cross Girder, Transverse Girder. A term applied to large timber members and to metal and reinforced concrete girder-like members placed generally perpendicular to and connected upon the main girders or trusses of a bridge span, including intermediate and end floor beams.

Cross Wall. See DIAPHRAGM WALL.

Crown of Roadway. 1. The crest line of the convexed surface. 2. The vertical dimension describing the total amount the surface is convexed or raised from gutter to crest. This is sometimes termed the cross fall of roadway.

Culvert. A small bridge constructed entirely below the elevation of the roadway surface and having no part or portion integral therewith. Structures over 20 feet in span parallel to the roadway are usually called bridges, rather than culverts; and structures less than 20 feet in span are called culverts even though they support traffic loads directly.

Curb. A stone, concrete or wooden barrier paralleling the side limit of the roadway to guide the movement of vehicle wheels and safeguard bridge trusses, railings or other constructions existing outside the roadway limit and also pedestrian traffic upon sidewalks from collision with vehicles and their loads.

Curb Inlet. See SCUPPER.

Curtain Wall. A term commonly applied to a thin masonry wall not designed to support superimposed loads either vertically or transversely.

A thin vertically placed and integrally built portion of the paving slab of a culvert intended to protect the culvert against undermining by stream scour. A similar construction placed in an inclined position is termed an "apron wall" or "apron."

A wall uniting the pillar or shaft portions of a dumbbell pier. However, its service function is that of a frame composed of struts and braces rendering the entire structure integral in its action. As here applied the term is synonymous with "diaphragm wall."

Curve Banking. See SUPERELEVATION.

Curves in Plan and Profile. A roadway may be curved in its lateral alignment, its vertical contour, or in both alignment and contour combined. The primary curves are described as:

1. Horizontal Curve. A curve in the plan location defining the alignment.

2. Vertical Curve. A curve in the profile location defining the elevation.

Cut. (*Cutting.*) That portion of a highway, railway, canal, ditch or other artificial construction of similar character produced by the removal of the natural formation of earth or rock whether sloped or level. The general terms "side hill cut" and "through cut" are used to describe the resulting cross sections of the excavations commonly encountered.

Cut Slope. A term applied to the inclined surface of an approach cut terminating in the ditch or gutter at its base, which in turn serves to remove accumulations of water from all areas drained into it.

Cylinder Pier. See PIER.

D

Dead Load. A static load due to the weight of the structure itself.

Dead Man. A general term applied to an anchorage member engaging the end of a stay rod, cable or other tie-like piece or part. The anchorage member is made secure through the resistance to movement produced by the earth, stone, brickbats, or other material used to embed and cover the anchor piece which may consist of a wooden log or timber, a metal beam or other structural shape, a quarried stone boulder or any other adaptable object. This type of anchor member is used to restrain and hold in position piles, bulkheads, cribs, and other constructions against horizontal movement as well as to resist the stresses of tie members acting in inclined and vertical directions.

Debris Rack. A grill type barrier used to intercept debris above a sewer or culvert inlet.

Deck. That portion of a bridge which provides direct support for vehicular and pedestrian traffic. The deck may be either a reinforced concrete slab, timber flooring, a steel plate or grating, or the top surface of abutting concrete members or units. While normally distributing load to a system of beams and stringers, a deck may also be the main supporting element of a bridge, as with a reinforced concrete slab structure or a laminated timber bridge.

Deck Bridge. A bridge having its floor elevation at, nearly at, or above the elevation of the uppermost portion of the superstructure.

Decking. A term specifically applied to bridges having wooden floors and used to designate the flooring only. It does not include the floor stringers, floor beams, or other members serving to support the flooring.

Deformation (elastic). Deformation occurring when stress in a material is less than the yield point. If the stress is removed, the material will return to its original shape.

Depth of Truss. As applied to trusses having parallel chords and to polygonal trusses having a midspan length with parallel chords; the vertical distance between the centerlines of action of the top and bottom chords.

Design Load. The loading comprising magnitudes and distributions of wheel, axle or other concentrations used in the determination of the stresses, stress distributions and ultimately the cross-sectional areas and compositions of the various portions of a bridge structure.

The design loading or loadings fixed by a specification are very commonly composite rather than actual, but are predicated upon a study of various types of vehicles. In lieu of a loading so determined for use as "standard," an equivalent uniform load designed to produce resulting structures practically identical with those evolved by the use of such loadings may be used. One or more concentrated loads may be used in conjunction with the uniform load to secure the effect corresponding to the incorporation of especially heavy vehicles within the normally maximum traffic considered as likely to pass upon a given bridge or a series of bridges. Such equivalent loadings are merely a convenience facilitating design operations.

In rating bridges for the Bridge Inspection Manual, either the H or HS trucks with their alternate lane loadings may be used. Or, if desired, the special legal limit trucks: Type 3, Type 3S 2, and Type 3–3, may be used.

Diagonal. See WEB MEMBERS.

Diagonal Stay. A cable support in a suspension bridge extending diagonally from the tower to the roadway system to add stiffness to the structure and diminish the deformations and undulations resulting from traffic service.

Diaphragm. A reinforcing plate or member placed within a member or deck system, respectively, to distribute stresses and improve strength and rigidity. See BRACING.

Diaphragm Wall (cross wall). A wall built transversely to the longitudinal centerline of a spandrel arch serving to tie together and reinforce the spandrel walls together with providing a support for the floor system in conjunction with the spandrel walls. To provide means for the making of inspections the diaphragms of an arch span may be provided with manholes.

The division walls of a reinforced concrete caisson dividing its interior space into compartments and reinforcing its walls. A wall serving to subdivide a box-like structure or portion of a structure into two or more compartments, or sections.

Dike. (*Dyke*). An earthen embankment constructed to provide a barrier to the inundation of an adjacent area which it encloses entirely or in part.

When used in conjunction with a bridge, its functions are commonly those of preventing stream erosion and localized scour and/or to so direct the stream current that debris will not accumulate upon bottom land adjacent to approach embankments, abutments, piers, towers, or other portions of the structure.

This term is occasionally misapplied to crib construction used to accomplish a like result. See CRIB.

Spur Dike. A projecting jetty-like construction placed adjacent to an abutment of the "U," "T," block or arched type upon the upstream and downstream sides, but sometimes only on the upstream side, to secure a gradual contraction of the stream width and induce a free even flow of water adjacent to and beneath a bridge. They may be constructed in extension of the wing wall or a winged abutment.

The common types of construction used for water wings are: (1) Wooden cribs filled with stones; (2) embankments riprapped on the waterway side; and (3) wooden and metal sheet piling.

Spur dikes serve to prevent stream scour and undermining of the abutment foundation and to relieve the condition which otherwise would tend to gather and hold accumulations of stream debris against and adjacent to the upstream side of the abutment.

Dimension Stone. A stone of relatively large dimensions, the face surface of which is either chisel or margin drafted but otherwise rough and irregular, commonly called either "rock face" or "quarry face."

Stones quarried with the dimensions large enough to provide cut stones with given finished dimensions.

Distribution Girder. A beam or girder-like member forming a part of the frame by which the dead and live loads are transmitted to the drum girder of a rim-bearing swing span.

Ditch. See DRAIN.

Diversion Drain. (*Diversion Flume.*) An open top paved drain constructed for the purpose of diverting and conveying water from a roadway gutter down the inclined surface of a bridge approach embankment or causeway.

Dolphin. A group or cluster of piles driven in one to two circles about a center pile and drawn together at their top ends around the center pile to form a buffer or guard for the protection of channel span piers or other portions of a bridge exposed to possible injury by collision with waterbound traffic. The tops of the piles are served with a wrapping consisting of several plies of wire, rope, coil, twist link, or stud link anchor chain, which, by being fastened at its ends only, renders itself taut by the adjustments of the piles resulting from service contact with ships, barges, or other craft. The center pile may project above the others to serve as a bollard for restraining and guiding the movements of water-borne traffic units.

Single steel and concrete piles of large size may also be used as dolphins.

Double Movable Bridge. A bridge in which the clear span for navigation is produced by joining the arms of two adjacent swing spans or the leaves of two adjacent bascule spans at or near the center of the navigable channel. The arms or leaves may act as cantilevers with a shear lock at their junction to provide for the passage of traffic over the joint. The leaves of bascules may be equipped to act as a hinged arch. Spans comprised of two bascule leaves are called double leaf bascule bridges. See MOVABLE BRIDGE.

Dowel. A short length of metal bar, either round or square, used to attach and prevent movement and displacement of wooden, stone, concrete, or metal pieces when placed in a bored, drilled, or cored hole located in their contact surfaces. A dowel may or may not be sized to provide a driving fit in the hole. In stone and premolded concrete structures the dowels are commonly set in lead, mortar, or other material filling the portions of the holes not occupied by the dowels. In concrete construction the plastic concrete is usually either placed around a dowel or the dowel is thrust into it.

In general, dowels function to resist shear forces, although footing dowels in reinforced concrete walls and columns resist bending forces.

Drain. (*Ditch, Gutter.*) A trench or trough-like excavation made to collect water. In general a drain is considered as functioning to collect and convey water whereas a ditch may only serve to collect it.

A gutter is a paved drain commonly constructed in conjunction with the curbs of the roadway or instead built closely adjacent to the paved portion of the roadway.

Drain Hole. (*Drip Hole.*) An aperture extending through a wall to provide an egress for water which might otherwise accumulate upon one of its sides. In this connection the term "weep hole" and "drain hole" are commonly used. See WEEP HOLE.

A cored, punched or bored hole in a box or trough shaped member or part to provide means for the egress of accumulated water or other liquid matter. In areas exposed to freezing temperatures, these holes are used to prevent damage by the expansive force incident to the freezing of water accumulations.

Drainage. The interception and removal of water from the roadway and/or sidewalk surfaces of a bridge or its approaches; from beneath the paved or otherwise prepared roadway and/or sidewalk surfaces of the approaches and from the sloped surfaces of hillsides, cuts, embankments, and causeways; from the backfill or other material in contact with abutments, retaining walls, counterweight wells or parts of a bridge or incidental structure.

A ditch, drain, gutter, gully, flume, catch basin, downspout, scupper, weep hole, or other construction or appliance facilitating the interception and removal of water.

Drainage Area, Catchment Area. The area from which the run-off water passing beneath a bridge or passing a specific location in a river or stream is produced.

Drawbridge. A general term applied to a bridge over a navigable stream, river, lake, canal, tidal inlet, gut or strait having a movable superstructure span of any type permitting the channel to be freed of its obstruction to navigation. A popular but imprecise term.

Probably the earliest use of a drawbridge was for military purposes, utilizing a single leaf hinged frame lifted up or let down by a comparatively simple manually operated mechanism.

Draw Rest. A support constructed upon a fender or guard pier and equipped with a latch block for holding a swing span in open position. This support may consist of a block of masonry, a rigid metal frame or other construction adapted to the service requirements.

Draw Span. A general term applied to either a swing or a retractile type movable superstructure span of a bridge over a navigable stream, river, lake, canal, tidal inlet, gut or strait. See MOVABLE BRIDGE.

Drift Bolt. A short length of metal bar, either round or square, used to connect and hold in position wooden members placed in contact. It may or may not be made with a head and a tapered point. Drift bolts are commonly driven in holes having a diameter slightly less than the bolts. This condition appears to be the recognized practical difference between a drift bolt and a dowel. The difference is more a matter of usage of terms rather than of functions to be performed.

Drip Bead. A channel or groove in the under side of a belt course, coping, or other protruding exposed portion of a masonry structure intended to arrest the downward flow of rain water and cause it to drip off free from contact with surfaces below the projection.

Drip Hole. See DRAIN HOLE.

Drop Inlet. A box-like construction commonly built integrally with the upstream end of a culvert with provision for the water to flow in at its top and to enter the culvert proper at its bottom or within its bottom portion. Vegetable or other material likely to become lodged in the culvert may be retained in the base portion of this receiving device by constructing its base to form a sump below the inlet elevation of the culvert. The culvert inlet may or may not be provided with a grating.

Drum Girder. (*Rim Girder.*) The circular plate girder forming a part of a swing bridge turntable transferring its loadings to the rollers and to the circular track upon which they travel. When the swing span is in "closed" position the drum girder track receives the superstructure dead and live loads and transmits these to the substructure bearing area beneath the track.

Ductility. The ability to withstand non-elastic deformation without rupture.

Dyke. See DIKE.

E

Efflorescence. A white deposit on concrete or brick caused by crystallization of soluble salts brought to the surface by moisture in the masonry.

Elastic Deformation. See DEFORMATION.

Elastomer. A natural or synthetic rubber-like material.

Electrolytic Corrosion. See CORROSION (ELECTROLYTIC).

Element. Metal Structures. An angle, beam, plate or other rolled, forged or cast piece of metal forming a part of a built piece. For Wooden Structures. A board, plank, joist, scantling or other fabricated piece forming a part of a built piece.

End Block. On a prestressed concrete beam, the thickening of the web or increase in beam width at the end to provide adequate anchorage bearing for the post-tensioning wires, rods, or strands.

End Hammer. The hammering action of an end lift device upon its pedestal or bearing plate resulting from the deflections and vibrations set up by the movements of traffic upon a swing span when the lifting device is improperly adjusted.

End Lift. The mechanism consisting of wedges, toggles, link-and-roller, rocker-and-eccentric or other devices combined with shafts, gears, or other operating parts requisite to remove the camber or "droop" of a swing span.

End Post. The end compression member of a truss, either vertical or inclined in position and extending from chord to chord, functioning to transmit the truss end shear to its end bearing.

Epoxy. A synthetic resin which cures or hardens by chemical reaction between components which are mixed together shortly before use.

Equalizer. A balance lever engaging the counterweight and the suspending cables of a vertical lift span as a means of adjustment and equalization of the stresses in the latter.

Equilibrium. In statics, the condition in which the forces acting upon a body are such that no external effect (or movement) is produced.

Equivalent Uniform Load. A load having a constant intensity per unit of its length producing an effect equal or practically equal to that of a live load consisting of vehicle axle or wheel concentrations spaced at varying distances apart, when used as a substitute for the latter in determining the stresses in a structure.

Expansion Bearing. A general term applied to a device or assemblage designed to transmit a reaction from one member or part of a structure to another and to permit the longitudinal movements resulting from temperature changes and superimposed loads without transmitting a horizontal force to the substructure.

The expansion bearing is designed to permit movement by overcoming sliding, rolling or other friction conditions. In general, provision is made for a movement equal to 1¼" in 100', thus providing for ordinary irregularities in field erection and adjustment.

Expansion Dam. The part of an expansion joint serving as an end form for the placing of concrete at a joint. Also applied to the expansion joint device itself.

Expansion Joint. A joint designed to provide means for expansion and contraction movements produced by temperature changes, loadings or other agencies.

Expansion Rocker. An articulated assemblage forming a part of the movable end of a girder or truss and facilitating the longitudinal movements resulting from temperature changes and superimposed loads. Apart from its hinge connection the rocker proper is a cast or built-up member consisting essentially of a circular segment integrally joined by a web-like portion to a hub fitted for hinge action either with a pin hole or by having its ends formed into trunnions. In its service operation the rocker is commonly supported upon a shoe plate or pedestal. Strictly speaking, this is a segment of a roller. A short cast or built-up member hinged at both ends, or instead hinged at one end and provided with a circular segment or spherical type bearing at the other to facilitate expansion and contraction on other longitudinal rotational movements.

Expansion Roller. A cylinder so mounted that by revolution it facilitates expansion, contraction or other movements resulting from temperature changes, loadings or other agencies.

Expansion Shoe. (*Expansion Pedestal.*) An expansion bearing member or assemblage designed to provide means for expansion and contraction or other longitudinal movements. In general, the term "shoe" is applied to an assemblage of structural plates or plate-like castings permitting movement by sliding while the term "pedestal" is used to describe assemblages of castings or built-up members securing a somewhat greater total depth and providing for movement either by sliding or by rolling.

The masonry plate or casting is commonly held in a fixed position by anchor bolts and the superimposed shoe plate or pedestal is free to move longitudinally upon it or upon intervening rollers but is restrained from transverse movement either by a rib and slot, by pintles, by anchorage or by anchorage in combination with one of the first two mentioned. The term "bed plate" is sometimes used to designate the bottom portion of the assemblage.

Extrados. (*Back.*) 1. The curved surface of an arch farthest from its longitudinal construction axis or axes. 2. The curve defining the exterior surface of an arch.

Eyebar. A member consisting of a rectangular bar body with enlarged forged ends or heads having holes through them for engaging connecting pins.

An adjustable eyebar is composed of two sections fitted with upset threaded ends engaging a sleevenut or a turnbuckle.

Eyebolt. (*Ringbolt.*) A bolt having a forged eye at one end used, when installed in a structure, to provide means for making fast the end of a cable, a hooked rod or other part or portion of the bridge, or instead to provide a means of anchorage for unrelated equipment or structures.

A ringbolt is essentially an eyebolt fitted with a ring to serve the same purpose as described above for an eyebolt with added articulation.

F

Face Stones. The stones exposed to view in the face surfaces of abutments, piers, arches, retaining walls or other stone structures.

Face Wall.
  Abutment. See BREAST WALL.
  Spandrel Arch Structure. The outermost spandrel walls providing the face surfaces of the completed structure. See SPANDREL ARCH.

Factor of Safety. A factor or allowance predicated by common engineering practice upon the failure stress or stresses assumed to exist in a structure or a member or part thereof. Its purpose is to provide a margin in the strength, rigidity, deformation and endurance of a structure or its component parts compensating for irregularities existing in structural materials and workmanship, uncertainties involved in mathematical analysis and stress distribution, service deterioration and other unevaluated conditions.

Falsework. A temporary wooden or metal framework built to support without appreciable settlement and deformation the weight of a structure during the period of its construction and until it becomes self-supporting. In general, the arrangement of its details are devised to facilitate the construction operations and provide for economical removal and the salvaging of material suitable for reuse.

Fascia. An outside, covering member designed on the basis of architectural effect rather than strength and rigidity although its function may involve both.

A light, stringer-like member spanning longitudinally between cantilever brackets which support large overhangs on girder or beam bridges.

Fascia Girder. As exposed outermost girder of a span sometimes treated architecturally or otherwise to provide an attractive appearance.

Fatigue. The tendency of a member to fail at a lower stress when subjected to cyclical loading than when subjected to static loading.

Felloe Guard. See WHEEL GUARD.

Fender. 1. A structure placed at an upstream location adjacent to a pier to protect it from the striking force, impact and shock of floating stream debris, ice floes, etc. This structure is sometimes termed an "ice guard" in latitudes productive of lake and river ice to form ice flows. 2. A structure commonly consisting of dolphins, capped and braced rows of piles or of wooden cribs either entirely or partially filled with rock ballast, constructed upstream and downstream from the center and end piers (or abutments) of a fixed or movable superstructure span to fend off water-borne traffic from collision with these substructure parts, and in the case of a swing span, with the span while in its open position.

Fender Pier. A pier-like structure which performs the same service as a fender but is generally more substantially built. These structures may be constructed entirely or in part of stone or concrete masonry. See GUARD PIER.

Field Coat. A coat of paint applied upon the priming or base coat or upon a coat subsequently applied and, generally, after the structure is assembled and its joints completely connected by bolts, rivets or welds. This application is quite commonly a part of the field erection procedure and is, therefore, termed field painting.

Fill. (*Filling.*) Material, usually earth, used for the purpose of raising or changing the surface contour of an area, or for constructing an embankment.

Filler (Filler Plate). In wooden and structural steel construction. A piece used primarily to fill a space beneath a batten, splice plate, gusset, connection angle, stiffener or other element.

Filler Metal. Metal prepared in wire, rod, electrode or other adaptable form to be fused with the structure metal in the formation of a weld.

Filler Plate. See FILLER.

Fillet. 1. A curved portion forming a junction of two surfaces which would otherwise intersect at an angle. 2. In metal castings and rolled structural shapes a fillet is used to disseminate and relieve the shrinkage or other stresses tending to overstress and, perhaps, rupture the junction material. In castings it may also provide means for movement to take place at locations where the rigidity of the mold would otherwise resist and obstruct this action. 3. In concrete construction the use of mitered fillets in internal corners of forms not only serves the purposes applying to castings but also facilitates both the placing of concrete and the subsequent removal of forms.

Fillet Weld. A weld joining intersecting members by depositing weld metal to form a near-triangular or fillet shaped junction of the surfaces of the members so joined. This weld serves to unite the intersecting surfaces of two elements of a member.

Filling. See FILL.

Finger Dam. Expansion joint in which the opening is spanned by meshing steel fingers or teeth.

Fish Belly. A term applied to a girder or a truss having its bottom flange or its bottom chord, as the case may be, constructed either haunched or bow-shaped with the convexity downward. See LENTICULAR TRUSS.

Fixed-Ended Arch. See VOUSSOIR ARCH.

Fixed Bearing. The plates, pedestals, or other devices designed to receive and transmit to the substructure or to another supporting member or structure the reaction stresses of a beam, slab, girder, truss, arch or other type of superstructure span.

The fixed bearing is considered as holding the so-termed "fixed end" of the structure rigidly in position, but in practice the clearance space commonly provided in the anchorage may permit a relatively small amount of movement.

Fixed Bridge. A bridge having its superstructure spans fixed in position except that provision may be made in their construction for expansion and contraction movements resulting from temperature changes, loadings, or other agencies.

Fixed Span. A superstructure span having its position practically immovable, as compared to a movable span.

Flange. The part of a rolled I-shaped beam or of a built-up girder extending transversely across the top and bottom edges of the web. The flanges are considered to carry the compressive and tensile forces that comprise the internal resisting moment of the beam, and may consist of angles, plates, or both.

Flange Angle. An angle used to form a flange element of a built-up girder, column, strut or similar member.

Floating Bridge. In general this term means the same as "Pontoon Bridge." However, its parts providing buoyancy and supporting power may consist of logs or squared timbers, held in position by lashing pieces, chains or ropes, and floored over with planks, or the bridge itself may be of hollow cellular construction.

Floating Foundation. A term sometimes applied to a "foundation raft" or "foundation grillage." Used to describe a soil-supported raft or mat foundation with low bearing pressures.

Flood Gate. (*Tide Gate.*) An automatically operated gate installed in a culvert or bridge waterway to prevent the ingress of flood or tide water to the area drained by the structure.

Floor. See DECK.

Floor Beam. A beam or girder located transversely to the general alignment of the bridge and having its ends framed upon the columns of bents and towers or upon the trusses or girders of superstructure spans. A floor beam at the extreme end of a girder or truss span is commonly termed an end floor beam.

Floor System. The complete framework of floor beams and stringers or other members supporting the bridge floor proper and the traffic loading including impact thereon.

Flow Line. The surface of a water course.

Flux. A material which prevents, dissolves, and removes oxides from metal during the welding process. It may be in the coating on a metal stick electrode or a granular mass covering the arc in submerged arc welding and protects the weld from oxidation during the fusion process.

Footbridge. (*Pedestrian Bridge.*) A bridge designed and constructed to provide means of traverse for pedestrian traffic only.

Footing. (*Footing Course, Plinth.*) The enlarged, or spread-out, lower portion of a substructure, which distributes the structure load either to the earth or to supporting piles. The most common footing is the concrete slab, although stone piers also utilize footings. Plinth refers to stone work as a rule. "Footer" is a local term for footing.

Foot Wall. See TOE WALL.

Forms. (*Form Work, Lagging, Shuttering.*) The constructions, either wooden or metal, providing means for receiving, molding and sustaining in position the plastic mass of concrete placed therein to the dimensions, outlines and details of surfaces planned for its integral parts throughout its period of induration or hardening.

The terms "forms" and "form work" are synonymous. The term "lagging" is commonly applied to the surface shaping areas of forms producing the intradoses of arches or other curved surfaces, especially when strips are used.

Forms. (SIP, Stay-in-Place.) A prefabricated metal concrete deck form that will remain in place after the concrete has set.

Form Work. See FORMS.

Foundation. The supporting material upon which the substructure portion of a bridge is placed. A foundation is "natural" when consisting of natural earth, rock or near-rock material having stability adequate to support the superimposed loads without lateral displacement or compaction entailing appreciable settlement or deformation. Also, applied in an imprecise fashion to a substructure unit.

Consolidated Soil Foundation. A foundation of soft soil rendered more resistant to its loads by (1) consolidating the natural material, (2) by the incorporation of other soil material (sand, gravel, etc.) into the soft material, and (3) by the injection of cementing materials into the soil mass which will produce consolidation by lapidification.

Pile or Piled Foundation. A foundation reinforced by driving piles in sufficient number and to a depth adequate to develop the bearing power required to support the foundation load.

Foundation Excavation. (*Foundation Pit.*) The excavation made to accommodate a foundation for a retaining wall, abutment, pier or other structure or element thereof.

Foundation Grillage. A construction consisting of steel, timber, or concrete members placed in layers. Each layer is normal to those above and below it and the members within a layer are generally parallel, producing a crib or grid-like effect. Grillages are usually placed under very heavy concentrated loads.

Foundation Load. The load resulting from traffic, superstructure, substructure, approach embankment, approach causeway, or other incidental load increment imposed upon a given foundation area.

Foundation Pile. A pile, whether of wood, reinforced concrete, or metal used to reinforce a foundation and render it satisfactory for the supporting of superimposed loads.

Foundation Pit. See FOUNDATION EXCAVATION.

Foundation Seal. A mass of concrete placed underwater within a cofferdam for the base portion of an abutment, pier, retaining wall or other structure to close or seal the cofferdam against incoming water from foundation springs, fissures, joints or other water carrying channels. See TREMIE.

Foundation Stone. The stone or one of the stones of a course having contact with the foundation of a structure.

Frame. A structure having its parts or members so arranged and secured that the entire assemblage may not be distorted when supporting the loads, forces, and physical pressures considered in its design. The framing of a truss relates to the design and fabrication of the joint assemblages.

Framing. The arrangement and manner of joining the component members of a bent, tower, truss, floor system or other portion of a bridge structure to insure a condition wherein each element and member may function in accord with the conditions attending its design. Framing must be interpreted as including both design and fabrication for the complete structure.

Friction Roller. A roller placed between parts or members intended to facilitate change in their relative positions by reducing the frictional resistance to translation movement.

Frost Heave. The upward movement of and force exerted by soil due to alternate freezing and thawing of retained moisture.

Frost Line. The depth to which soil may be frozen.

G

Galvanic Action. Electrical current between two unlike metals.

Gauge. The distance between parallel lines of rails, rivet holes, etc. A measure of thickness of sheet metal or wire.

Girder. A flexural member which is the main or primary support for the structure, and which usually receives loads from floor beams and stringers.

Any large beam, especially if built up.

Girder Bridge. A bridge whose superstructure consists of two or more girders supporting a separate floor system of slab and floor beams, or slab, stringer, and floor beam, as differentiated from a multi-beam bridge or a slab bridge.

Any bridge utilizing large, built-up steel beams, prestressed concrete beams, or concrete box girders.

With reference to the vertical location of the floor system, plate girder spans are divided into two types, viz.:

1. Through bridges having the floor system near the elevation of the bottom flanges, whereby traffic passes between the top flanges.

2. Deck bridges having the floor system at or above the elevation of the top flanges whereby traffic passes above the girders.

Girder Span. A span in which the major longitudinal supporting members are girders. It may be simple, cantilever or continuous in type.

Gothic Arch. (*Pointed Arch.*) An arch in which the intrados surface is composed of two equal cylinder segments intersecting obtusely at the crown.

The Tudor Arch is a modification of the Gothic, produced by the introduction of shorter radius cylinder segments at the haunches thus rendering it a four-centered form or type.

Grade Crossing. A term applicable to an intersection of two or more highways, two railroads or one railroad and one highway at a common grade or elevation; now commonly accepted as meaning the last of these combinations.

Grade Intersection. The location where a horizontal and an inclined length of roadway or, instead, two inclined lengths meet in profile. To provide an easy transition from one to the other they are connected by a vertical curve and the resulting profile is a sag or a summit depending upon whether concaved or convexed upward.

Grade Separation. A term applied to the use of a bridge structure and its approaches to divide or separate the crossing movement of vehicular, pedestrian or other traffic, by confining portions thereof to different elevations. See OVERPASS.

Gradient. The rate of inclination of the roadway and/or sidewalk surface(s) from horizontal applying to a bridge and its approaches. It is commonly expressed as a percentage relation of horizontal to vertical dimensions.

Gravity Wall. See RETAINING WALL.

Grillage. A platform-like construction or assemblage used to insure distribution of loads upon unconsolidated soil material. See FOUNDATION GRILLAGE.

A frame composed of I-beams or other structural shapes rigidly connected and built into a masonry bridge seat, skewback or other substructure support to insure a satisfactory distribution of the loads transmitted by the superstructure shoes, pedestals, or other bearing members.

Grout. A mortar having a sufficient water content to render it a free-flowing mass, used for filling (grouting) the interstitial spaces between the stones or the stone fragments (spalls) used in the "backing" portion of stone masonry; for fixing anchor bolts and for filling cored spaces in castings, masonry, or other spaces where water may accumulate.

Guard Pier. (*Fender Pier.*) A pier-like structure built at right angles with the alignment of a bridge or at an angle therewith conforming to the flow of the stream current and having adequate length, width, and other provisions to protect the swing span in its open position from collision with passing vessels or other water-borne equipment and materials. It also serves to protect the supporting center pier of the swing span from injury and may or may not be equipped with a rest pier upon which the swing span in its open position may be latched. The type of construction varies with navigation and stream conditions from a simple pile and timber structure or a wooden crib-stone ballasted structure to a solid masonry one, or to a combination construction. In locations where ice floes or other water-borne materials may accumulate upon the upstream pier end, a cutwater or a starling is an essential detail. See FENDER PIER.

Guard Railing. (*Guard Rail, Guard Fence, Protection Railing.*) A fencelike barrier or protection built within the roadway shoulder area and intended to function as a combined guide or guard for the movement of vehicular and/or pedestrian traffic and to prevent or hinder the accidental passage of such traffic beyond the berm line of the roadway.

Guide. A member or element of a member functioning to hold in position and direct the movement of a moving part.

Guide Roller. A roller fixed in its location or position and serving both as a friction roller and as a pilot or guide for a part or member in contact with it.

Gusset. A plate serving to connect or unite the elements of a member or the members of a structure and to hold them in correct alignment and/or position at a joint. A plate may function both as a gusset and splice plate while under other conditions it may function as a gusset and stay plate. See SPLICE PLATE and STAY PLATE.

Gutter. See DRAIN.

Gutter Grating. A perforated or barred cover placed upon an inlet to a drain to prevent the entrance of debris gathered and brought to the inlet by the water stream.

Guy. A cable, chain, rod or rope member serving to check and control undulating, swaying or other movements, or to hold a fixed alignment or position a structure or part thereof by having one of its ends bolted, clamped, tied or otherwise fastened upon it, the other end being secured upon a part or member of the structure or upon a disconnected anchorage.

H

H-Beam. (*H-Pile.*) A rolled steel bearing pile having an H-shaped cross section.

Hand Hole. Holes provided in cover plates of built-up box sections to permit access to the interior for maintenance and construction purposes.

Hand Operated Span. A manpower-operated movable span to which the force for operating is applied upon a capstan, winch, windlass or wheel.

The terms "Hand Draw Bridge," "Hand Swing Bridge" and "Lever Swing Bridge" are applied to swing spans of hand-operated type.

Hand Rail. See RAILING.

Hanger. A tension element or member serving to suspend or support a member attached thereto. A tension member, whether a rod, eyebar, or built-up member supporting a portion of the floor system of a truss, arch or suspension span. In suspension bridge construction wire cable is used and the complete member is commonly termed a "suspender."

Haunch. A deepening of a beam or column, the depth usually being greatest at the support and vanishing towards or at the center. The curve of the lower flange or surface may be circular, elliptic, parabolic, straight or stepped.

Head. A measure of water pressure expressed in terms of an equivalent weight or pressure exerted by a column of water. The height of the equivalent column of water is the head.

Headwater. The depth of water at the inlet end of a pipe, culvert, or bridge waterway.

Headway. See CLEAR HEADWAY.

Heat Treatment. Any of a number of various operations involving heating and cooling that are used to impart specific properties to metals. Examples are tempering, quenching, annealing, etc.

Heel of Span. The rotation end of a bascule span.

Heel Stay. See SHEAR LOCK.

Hemispherical Bearing. A bearing which utilizes the ball and socket principle by having male and female spherical segments forming the bearing areas or surfaces of the interlocking elements, thus providing for movements by revolution in any direction.

In order to insure accurate adjustment of the mating elements it is essential that a pintle or other self-centering device be provided as a part of the construction details.

Hinged Joint. A joint constructed with a pin, cylinder segment, spherical segment or other device permitting movement by rotation.

Hip Joint. (*The Hip of Truss.*) The juncture of the inclined end post with the end top chord member of a truss. In the truss of a swing span, the juncture of the inclined end post located adjacent to the center of span, with the combined top chord and the connecting tie member between the swing span arms, is designated an "interior hip joint" or an "interior hip of truss."

Hip Vertical. The vertically placed tension member engaging the hip joint of a truss and supporting the first panel floor beam in a through truss span, or instead, only the bottom chord in a deck truss span.

Hook Bolt. 1. A bolt having a forged hook at one end used for essentially the same purposes as described for an eyebolt. See EYEBOLT. 2. A bolt having its head end bent at or nearly at a right angle with its body portion and, when in use, acting as a clamp.

Howe Truss. A truss of the parallel chord type originally adapted to wooden bridge construction but with the later development of metal bridge trusses it was adopted only to a limited extent due to the uneconomical use of metal in its compression members. The web system is composed of vertical(tension) rods at the panel points with an X pattern of diagonals.

Hydrolysis. A chemical process of decomposition in the presence of elements of water.

Hydroplaning. Loss of contact between a tire and the deck surface when the tire planes or glides on a film of water covering the deck.

I

Ice Guard. See FENDER.

Impact. As applied to bridge design—a dynamic increment of stress equivalent in magnitude to the difference between the stresses produced by a static load when quiescent and by a load moving in a straight line.

Impact Load. (*Impact Allowance.*) A load allowance or increment intended to provide for the dynamic effect of a load applied in a manner other than statically.

Indeterminate Stress. A stress induced by the incorporation of a redundant member in a truss or of an additional reaction in a beam rendering stress distributions indeterminate by the principles of statics.

In redundant beams or trusses the distribution of the stresses depends upon the relative stiffnesses or areas of the members.

Inelastic Compression. See COMPRESSION (INELASTIC).

Inspection Ladders. (*Inspection Platforms and Walks.*) Special devices or appliances designed to afford a safe and efficient means for making inspections and tests to determine the physical condition of a structure and to facilitate repair operations incident to its maintenance which must include these service conveniences. To prevent displacement they will be, in general, **rigidly** fixed upon the structure. However, **certain** types of structures are adapted to the use of movable platform devices for suspension from the railings or other parts which are or may be adapted thereto.

The term "catwalk" is applied to narrow permanent walks supported, usually, by brackets or by hangers and located below and/or above the bridge floor. This term is also applied to temporary walks used in the construction of suspension and other types of bridges as utilities facilitating the movements of labor and materials, and the supervision and inspection operations.

Intercepting Ditch. A ditch constructed to prevent surface water from flowing in contact with the toe of an embankment or causeway or down the slope of a cut.

Intergranular Pressure. Pressure between soil grains.

Intermittent Weld. A noncontinuous weld commonly composed of a series of short welds with intervening spaces arranged with fixed spacing and length.

Intrados. (*Soffit.*) The curved surface of an arch nearest its longitudinal (constructional) axis or axes. Properly speaking the intrados is the curve defining the interior surface of the arch.

J

Jack Stringer. The outermost stringer supporting the bridge floor in a panel or bay. It is commonly of less strength than a main stringer.

Joint. In Stone Masonry. The space between individual stones.

In Concrete Construction. The divisions or terminations of continuity produced at predetermined locations or by the completion of a period of construction operations. These may or may not be open.

In a Truss or Frame Structure. (1) A point at which members of a truss or frame are joined, (2) the composite assemblage of pieces or members around or about the point of intersection of their lines of action in a truss or frame.

K

Keystone. A stone of the crown string course of an arch. However, this term is most commonly applied to the symmetrically shaped wedge-like stone located in a head ring course at the crown of the arch, which thus exposed to view produces desired architectural effects. This head ring stone commonly extends short distances above and below the extradosal and intradosal limits of the voussoirs of adjoining string courses. The final stone placed, thereby closing the arch.

King-Post. (*King Rod.*) The post member in a "King-post" type truss or in a "King-post" portion of any other type of truss.

King-Post Truss. A truss adapted to either wooden or metal bridge construction. It is composed of two triangular panels with a common vertical. A beam or chord extends the full truss length.

In the through form of this truss the inclined members are struts and the vertical or King-post is a hanger. In the deck truss, the two inclined members become tie (tension) members and the vertical becomes a post (compression) member.

The King-post truss is the simplest of trusses belonging to the triangular system. However, it is described with equal accuracy as a trussed girder.

K-Truss. A truss having a web system wherein the diagonal members intersect the vertical members at or near the mid-height. When thus arranged the assembly in each panel forms a letter "K"; hence the name "K-Truss."

Knee Brace. A member usually short in length, engaging at its ends two other members which are joined to form a right angle or a near-right angle. It thus serves to strengthen and render more rigid the connecting joint.

Knee Wall. A return of the abutment backwall at its ends to enclose the bridge seat on three of its sides. The returned ends may or may not serve to retain a portion of the bridge approach material, but do hide the bridge seat, beam ends, and bearings.

Knuckle. An appliance forming a part of the anchorage of a suspension bridge main suspension member permitting free longitudinal movement of the anchorage chain at locations where it changes its direction and providing for elastic deformations induced by temperature changes and the pull exerted by the suspension member.

L

Lacing. See LATTICE.

Ladle Analysis. (*Ladle Test, Check Analysis.*) As applied to the chemical determination of the constituents of steel or other ferrous metals, the terms "ladle analysis" and "ladle test" are synonymous and are used to designate the analysis of drillings or chips taken from the small ingot or ingots cast from a spoon sample taken from each melt during the pouring (teeming) operation.

The term "check analysis" is applied to the analysis of drillings taken from the finished material after being rolled, forged or otherwise worked. It is primarily intended as a check determination of the results secured from the ingots made at the furnace. Specifications may provide a tolerance or margin of variation between the ingot and the finished material analyses.

Lagging. See FORMS.

Laminated Timber. Timber planks glued together to form a larger member. Laminated timber is used for frames, arches, beams, and columns.

Lap Joint. A joint in which a splice is secured by fixing two elements or members in a position wherein they project upon or overlap each other.

Latch. (*Latch Block.*) The device or mechanism commonly provided at one or both ends of a swing span to hold the span in its correct alignment when in its closed position, and in readiness for the application of the end wedges or lifts.

Latch Lever. A hand-operated lever attached by a rod, cable or chain to the latching device of a movable span and used to engage and to release the latch.

Lateral Bracing. (*Lateral System.*) The bracing assemblage engaging the chords and inclined end posts of truss and the flanges of plate girder spans in the horizontal or inclined planes of these members to function in resisting the transverse forces resulting from wind, lateral vibration, and traffic movements tending to produce lateral movement and deformation. See BRACING.

Lattice. (*Latticing, Lacing.*) An assemblage of bars, channels, or angles singly or in combination bolted, riveted or welded in inclined position upon two or more elements of a member to secure them in correct position and assure their combined action. When the bars form a double system by being inclined in opposite directions the assemblage is termed "double lattice." When so arranged the bars are commonly connected at their intermediate length intersections.

Lattice Truss. In general, a truss having its web members inclined but more commonly the term is applied to a truss having two or more web systems composed entirely of diagonal members at any interval and crossing each other without reference to vertical members. Vertical members when used perform the functions of web stiffeners. They may be utilized for connecting vertically placed brace frames to the girders.

Leaf. The portion of a bascule bridge which forms the span or a portion of the span of the structure.

Ledge Course. In masonry or concrete construction, a course forming a projection beyond the plane of a superimposed course or courses. The projecting portion may be wash dressed to permit an unobstructed flow of rain water down the wall surface. A ledge course differs from a belt or string course in having a projection only upon its topmost bed. This construction is also known as a "Ledger Course."

Ledge Rock. See BED ROCK.

Lenticular Truss. (*Fish Belly Truss.*) A truss having polygonal top and bottom chords curved in opposite directions with their ends meeting at a common joint. The chords nearly coincide with parabolic arcs. In through spans the floor system is suspended from the joints of the bottom chord and the end posts are vertical.

Lifting Girder. A girder or girder-like member engaging the trusses or girders of a vertical lift span and to which the suspending cables are attached.

Lift Span. A superstructure span moved by revolution in a vertical plane or by lifting in a vertical direction to free a navigable waterway of the obstruction it presents to navigation. See MOVABLE BRIDGE.

Link and Roller. An adjustable device or assemblage consisting of a hinged strut-like link fitted with a roller at its bottom end, supported upon a shoe plate or pedestal and operated by a thrust strut serving to force it into a vertical position and to withdraw it therefrom. When installed at each outermost end of the girders or the trusses of a swing span their major function is to lift them to an extent that their camber or droop will be removed and the arms rendered free to act as simple spans. When the links are withdrawn to an inclined position fixed by the operating mechanism the span is free to be moved to an open position.

Lintel Bridge. A bridge having a single span or a series of spans composed of slabs of stone or reinforced concrete spanning the interval or intervals between its substructure elements.

Lintel Stone. A stone used to support a wall over an opening.

Live Load. A dynamic load such as traffic load that is supplied to a structure suddenly or that is accompanied by vibration, oscillation or other physical condition affecting its intensity.

Loading Girder. A term applied to the girder or girders of a center bearing type swing span, located above the pivot pier and functioning to concentrate the superimposed load upon the pivot.

Location. The longitudinal line assumed for construction purposes, which may or may not coincide with the center line of bridge; together with the gradients upon the bridge and its approaches established upon the construction plans and/or on the bridge site preparatory to construction operations.

Lock Device. A mechanism which locks the movable span of a bridge in its "closed" position and prevents movement to "open" position until released. The device on a swing span may also be used to lock the span in its "open" position at times when wind or other conditions render this prevention of movement desirable.

Locking Mechanism. A general term applied to the various devices used for holding in their closed or traffic service position a bascule, vertical lift or swing span of any type. This term applies not only to the locking or latching appliance but includes also the levers, shafts, gears or other parts incidental to their service operation.

Longitudinal Bracing. (*Longitudinal System.*) The bracing assemblage engaging the columns of trestle and viaduct bents and towers in perpendicular or slightly inclined planes located lengthwise with the bridge structure and functioning to resist the longitudinal forces resulting from traffic traction and momentum, wind or other forces tending to produce longitudinal movement and deformation. See BRACING.

M

Margin. See TOLERANCE.

Masonry. A general term applying to abutments, piers, retaining walls, arches and allied structures built of stone, brick or concrete and known correspondingly as stone, brick or concrete masonry.

Masonry Plate. A steel plate or a plate-shaped member whether cast, rolled or forged, built into or otherwise attached upon an abutment, pier, column, or other substructure part to support the rocker, shoe, or pedestal of a beam, girder or truss span and to distribute the load to the masonry beneath.

Mattress. A mat-like protective covering composed of brush and poles, commonly willow, compacted by wire or other lashings and ties and placed upon river and stream beds and banks; lake, tidal or other shores to prevent erosion and scour by water movement action.

Meander. The tortuous channel that characterizes the serpentine curvature of a slow flowing stream in a flood plain.

Member. An individual angle, beam, plate forging, casting or built piece, with or without connected parts for joints, intended ultimately to become an integral part of an assembled frame or structure.

Milled. In steel fabrication, a careful grinding of an edge or surface to assure good bearing or fit.

Mortar. An intimate mixture, in a plastic condition, of cement, or other cementitious material with fine aggregate and water, used to bed and bind together the quarried stones, bricks, or other solid materials composing the major portion of a masonry construction or to produce a plastic coating upon such constructions.

The indurated jointing material filling the interstices between and holding in place the quarried stones or other solid materials of masonry construction. Correspondingly, this term is applied to the cement coating used to produce a desired surface condition upon masonry constructions and is described as the "mortar finish," "mortar coat," "floated face or surface," "parapet," etc.

The component of concrete composed of cement, or other indurating material with sand and water when the concrete is a mobile mass and correspondingly this same component after it has attained a rigid condition through hardening of its cementing constituents.

Movable Bridge. A bridge of any type having one or more spans capable of being raised, turned, lifted, or slid from its normal vehicular and/or pedestrian service location to provide for the passage of navigation. The movements of the superstructure may be produced either manually or by engine power.

Bascule Bridge. A bridge having a superstructure designed to swing vertically about a fixed or a moving horizontal axis. The axis may be the center of a hinge pin or trunnion, or it may be only a line fixing the center of a circular rotation combined with translation, (rolling lift bridge).

Vertical Lift Bridge. A bridge having a superstructure designed to be lifted vertically by cables or chains attached to the ends of the movable span and operating over sheaves placed upon the tops of masts or towers or by other mechanical devices functioning to lift the span to "open" position and to lower it into its "closed" position with its ends seated upon bridge seat pedestals.

Pontoon Bridge. A bridge ordinarily composed of boats, scows or pontoons so connected to the deck or floor construction that they are retained in position and serve to support vehicular and pedestrian traffic. A pontoon bridge may be so constructed that a portion is removable and thus serve to facilitate navigation. Modern floating bridges may have pontoons built integrally with the deck.

Retractile Draw Bridge. (*Traverse Draw Bridge.*) A bridge having a superstructure designed to move horizontally either longitudinally or diagonally from "closed" to "open" position, the portion acting in cantilever being counterweighted by that supported upon rollers.

Rolling Lift Bridge. A bridge of the bascule type devised to roll backward and forward upon supporting girders when operated throughout an "open and closed" cycle.

Swing Bridge. A bridge having a superstructure designed to revolve in a horizontal plane upon a pivot from its "closed" position to an "open" one wherein its alignment is normal or nearly normal to the original alignment. For a structure having its substructure skewed the design commonly provides for revolution in one direction only and through an arc less than 90°. The superstructure is balanced upon a center and its ends acting as cantilevers when the end bearings are released may be either equal in length or unequal with the shorter one counterweighted to permit free revolution movement. A swing bridge with its end bearings released may be supported: (1) upon a single center bearing; (2) upon a circular rim or drum supported upon rollers and (3) upon a center bearing and rim in combination.

Movable Span. A general term applied to a superstructure span designed to be withdrawn, swung, lifted or otherwise moved longitudinally, horizontally or vertically to free a navigable waterway of the obstruction it presents to navigation.

Mud Sill. A single piece of timber or a unit composed of two or more timbers placed upon a soil foundation as a support for a single column, a framed trestle bent, or other similar member of a structure.

A load distribution piece aligned with and placed directly beneath the sill piece of a framed bent is termed a "Sub-sill" although it may serve also as a mud sill.

N

N-Truss. See PRATT TRUSS.

Natural Slope. See ANGLE OF REPOSE.

Neat Line. (*Neat Surface.*) The general alignment position or the general surface position of a face or other surface exlusive or regardless of the projections of individual stones, belts, belt courses, copings or other incidental or ancillary projections in a masonry structure.

Neutral Axis. The axis of a member in bending along which the strain is zero. On one side of the neutral axis the fibers are in tension, on the other side in compression.

Normal Roadway Cross Section. The roadway cross section with its crown in countradistinction to the superelevated cross sections used upon horizontal curves of different degrees of curvature and the transition lengths required for their development.

Nose. A projection acting as a cut water on the upstream end of a pier. See STARLING.

Notch Effect. Stress concentration caused by an abrupt discontinuity or change in section. Such concentrations may have a marked effect on fatigue strength of a member.

O

Operator's House. (*Operator's Cabin.*) The building containing the power plant and operating machinery and devices required for the operator's (bridge tender's) work in executing the complete cycle of opening and closing a movable bridge span.

Overpass. (*Underpass.*) The applications of these terms are definitely indicated by their constructions. For any given combination of highways, railways, and canals, the basic element is a separation of grades. The use of these terms is fixed by the relative elevations of the traffic ways involved; for the lower roadway, the structure is an underpass; for the upper roadway, an overpass.

P

Packing Ring. See SEPARATOR.

Paddleboard. Striped, paddle-shaped signs or boards placed on the roadside in front of a narrow bridge as a warning.

Panel. (*Sub-Panel.*) The portion of a truss span between adjacent points of intersection of web and chord members and, by common practice, applied to intersections upon the bottom chord. A truss panel divided into two equal or unequal parts by an intermediate web member, generally by a subdiagonal or a hanger, forms the panel division commonly termed "subpanels."

Panel Point. The point of intersection of primary web and chord members of a truss.

Parabolic Truss. (*Parabolic Arched Truss.*) A polygonal truss having its top chord and end post vertices coincident with the arc of a parabola; its bottom chord straight and its web system either triangular or quadrangular.

Parapet. A wall-like member composed of brick, stone or reinforced concrete construction upon the retaining wall portion of an approach cut, embankment or causeway or along the outermost edge of the roadway or the sidewalk portion of a bridge to serve as a protection to vehicular and/or pedestrian traffic. While the terms balustrade and parapet are used, in a measure, synonymously, the latter is commonly regarded as applying to barriers of the block type without openings within the body portion. See BALUSTRADE.

Parker Truss. See PRATT TRUSS.

Pedestal. A cast or built-up metal member or assemblage functioning primarily to transmit load from one member or part of a structure to another member or part. A secondary function may be to provide means for longitudinal, transverse or revolution movements.

A block-like construction of stone, concrete or brick masonry placed upon the bridge seat of an abutment or pier to provide a support for the ends of the beams.

Pedestrian Bridge. See FOOT BRIDGE.

Penetration. When Applied to Creosoted Lumber. The depth to which the surface wood is permeated by the creosote oil.

When Applied to Welding. The depth to which the surface metal of the structure part (Structure metal) is fused and coalesced with the fused weld metal to produce a weld joint. See WELD PENETRATION.

When Applied to Pile Driving. The depth a pile tip is driven into the ground.

Pier. A structure composed of stone, concrete, brick, steel or wood and built in shaft or block-like form to support the ends of the spans of a multi-span superstructure at an intermediate location between its abutments.

The following types of piers are adapted to bridge construction. The first three are functional distinctions, while the remaining types are based upon form or shape characteristics.

Anchor Pier. A pier functioning to resist an uplifting force, as for example: The end reaction of the anchor arm of a cantilever bridge. This pier functions as a normal pier structure when subjected to certain conditions of superstructure loading.

Pivot Pier. Center Pier. A term applied to the center bearing pier supporting a swing span while operating throughout an opening-closing cycle. This pier is commonly circular in shape but may be hexagonal, octagonal or even square in plan.

Rest Pier. A pier supporting the end of a movable bridge span when in its closed position.

Cylinder Pier. A type of pier produced by sinking a cylindrical steel shell to a desired depth and filling it with concrete. The foundation excavation may be made by open dredging within the shell and the sinking of the shell may proceed simultaneously with the dredging.

Dumbbell Pier. A pier consisting essentially of two cylindrical or rectangular shaped piers joined by a web constructed integrally with them.

Hammerhead Pier. (*Tee Pier.*) A pier with a cylindrical or rectangular shaft, and a relatively long, transverse cap.

Pedestal Pier. A structure composed of stone, concrete or brick built in block-like form—supporting a column of a bent or tower of a viaduct. Foundation conditions or other practical considerations may require that two or more column supports be placed upon a single base or footing section. To prevent accumulation of stream debris at periods of high water or under other conditions the upstream piers may be constructed with cut-waters and in addition the piers may be connected by an integrally built web between them. When composed only of a wide blocklike form, it is called a wall or solid pier.

Pile Pier or Bent. A pier composed of driven piles capped or decked with a timber grillage or with a reinforced concrete slab forming the bridge seat.

Rigid Frame Pier. Pier with two or more columns and a horizontal beam on top constructed to act like a frame.

Pier Cap. (*Pier Top.*) The topmost portion of a pier. On rigid frame piers, the term applies to the beam across the column tops. On hammerhead and tee piers, the cap is a continuous beam.

Pilaster. A column-like projection upon a face surface rarely intended to serve as a structural member but instead functioning as an architectural treatment to relieve the blankness of a plane surface.

Pile. A rod or shaft-like linear member of timber, steel, concrete, or composite materials driven into the earth to carry structure loads thru weak strata of soil to those strata capable of supporting such loads. Piles are also used where loss of earth support due to scour is expected.

Bearing Pile. One which receives its support in bearing through the tip (or lower end) of the pile.

Friction Pile. One which receives its support through friction resistance along the lateral surface of the pile.

Sheet Piles. Commonly used in the construction of bulkheads, cofferdams, and cribs to retain earth and prevent the inflow of water, liquid mud, and fine grained sand with water, are of three general types, viz.: (1) Timber composed of a single piece or of two or more pieces spiked or bolted together to produce a compound piece either with a lap or a tongued and grooved effect. (2) Reinforced concrete slabs constructed with or without lap or tongued and grooved effect. (3) Rolled steel shapes with full provision for rigid interlocking of the edges.

Pile Cap. Concrete footings for a pier or abutment supported on piles. Also applied to the concrete below the pile tops when footing reinforcing steel is placed completely above the piles.

Pile Cut-Off. The portion of a pile removed or to be removed from its driven butt end to secure the elevation specified or indicated.

Pile Shoe. A metal piece fixed upon the point or penetration end of a pile to protect it from injury in driving and to facilitate penetration in every dense earth material.

Pile Splice. One of the means of joining one pile upon the end of another to provide greater penetration length.

Piling. (*Sheet Piling.*) General terms applied to assemblages of piles in a construction. See PILE.

Pin. A cylindrical bar used as a means of connecting, holding in position, and transmitting the stresses of, the members forming a truss or a framed joint. To restrain the pin against longitudinal movement its ends are fitted with pin nuts, cotter bolts, or both. The nuts are commonly of the recessed type taking bearing at their edges upon the assemblage of members. To prevent the loosening of the nuts and the displacement of the pins by vibration, joint movements, and other service conditions, the pin ends may be burred or they may be fitted with cotters.

Pin-Connected Truss. A general term applied to a truss of any type having its chord and web members connected at the truss joints by pins.

Pinion. The small driving gear on the powertrain of a movable bridge.

Pinion Bracket. The frame supporting the turning pinion with its shaft and bearings upon the drum girder or the loading girder of a swing span.

Pin Joint. A joint in a truss or other frame in which the members are assembled upon a cylindrical pin.

Pin Packing. An arrangement of truss members on a pin at a pinned joint.

Pin Plate. A plate or shape riveted or otherwise rigidly attached upon the end of a member to secure a desired bearing upon a pin or pin-like bearing; to develop and distribute the stress of the joint and/or secure additional strength and rigidity in the member.

Pintle. A small steel pin or stud, engaging the rocker in an exansion bearing, thereby permitting rotation, transferring shear, and preventing translation.

Pitch. The longitudinal spacing between rivets, studs, bolts, holes, etc., which are arranged in a straight line.

Plate Girder. An I-shaped beam composed of a solid plate web with either flange plates or flange angles bolted, riveted or welded upon its edges. Additional cover plates may be attached to the flanges to provide greater flange area.

Plinth. See FOOTING.

Plinth Course. The course or courses of stone forming the base portion of an abutment, pier, parapet or retaining wall and having a projection or extension beyond the general surface of the main body of the structure. See also BASE and FOOTING.

Plug Weld. (*Slot Weld.*) A weld joining two elements of a member or two members so assembled that an area of contact will be secured and the weld produced by depositing weld metal within circular, square, slotted or other shaped holes cut through one or more of the elements or members. This weld serves to unite the elements of a member or to join the members intersecting at truss at other joints of a structure.

Pointed Arch. See GOTHIC ARCH.

Pointing. The operations incident to the compacting of the mortar in the outermost portion of a joint and the troweling or other treatment of its exposed surface to secure water tightness or desired architectural effect or both.

Polygonal Truss. A general term applied to a truss of any type having an irregular or "broken" alignment of straight top chord members which forms with the end posts and the bottom chord the perimeter of a polygon.

Pony Truss. A general term applied to a truss having insufficient height to permit the use of an effective top chord system of lateral bracing above the bridge floor.

Pop-Out. Conical fragment broken out of concrete surface. Normally about one inch in diameter. Shattered aggregate particles usually found at bottom of hole.

Portable Bridge. A bridge so designed and constructed that it may be readily erected for a temporary communication-transport service; disassembled and its members again reassembled and the entire structure rendered ready for further service.

Portal. The clear unobstructed space of a through bridge forming the entrance to the structure.

The entire portal member of the top chord bracing which fixes the uppermost limit of the vertical clearance. See BRACING. The portal of a skew bridge is described as a "skew portal."

Post. A term commonly applied to a relatively short member resisting compressive stresses, located vertical or nearly vertical to the bottom chord of a truss and common to two truss panels. Sometimes used synonymously for column. See COLUMN.

Posted. A limiting dimension, speed, or loading, e.g., posted load, posted clearance, posted speed, indicating larger dimensions and higher speeds and loads can not be safely taken by the bridge.

Pot Holes. Small worn or distintegrated areas of bridge floor or approach surface concaved by the wearing action of vehicle wheels.

Pratt Truss. (*N-Truss.*) A truss with parallel chords and a web system composed of vertical posts with diagonal ties inclined outward and upward from the bottom chord panel points toward the ends of the truss except the counters required in midlength panels. The Parker Truss is an adaptation of the Pratt Truss by making the top chord polygonal in shape.

Priming Coat. (*Base Coat.*) The first coat of paint applied to the metal or other material of a bridge. For metal structures this is quite commonly a fabricating shop application and is, therefore, termed the "shop coat."

Protection Fence. See GUARD RAILING.

Protection Railing. See GUARD RAILING.

Q

Queen-Post Truss. A parallel chord type of truss adapted to either timber or metal bridge construction, having three panels with one of the chords occupying only the length of the center panel. Unless center panel diagonals are provided, it is a trussed beam.

R

Rack. A bar with teeth on one of its sides, designed to mesh with the gears of a pinion or worm. The rack is usually attached to the moving portion of a movable bridge and receives the motive power from the pinion.

Radial Rod. (*Spider Rod.*) A radially located tie rod connecting the roller circle of a rim-bearing swing span with the center pivot or center bearing casting.

Radial Strut. A radially located brace member of the drum construction of a rim-bearing swing span.

Railing. (*Handrail.*) A wooden, brick, stone, concrete or metal fence-like construction built at the side of the roadway, or the sidewalk, upon the retaining wall portion of an approach cut, embankment, or causeway or at the outermost edge of the roadway or the sidewalk portion of a bridge to guard or guide the movement of both pedestrian and vehicular traffic and to prevent the accidental passage of traffic over the side of the structure.

The term "handrail" is commonly applied only to railing presenting a latticed, barred, balustered or other open web construction.

Rake. The slope, batter or inclination from a horizontal, vertical or other assumed plane, of the sides of an embankment or other inclined earth construction; the batter of a face or other surface of masonry; of the plane of a truss side of a tower or other portion of a bridge superstructure or of any member thereof.

Ramp. An inclined traffic-way leading from one elevation to another. The general term used to designate an inclined roadway and/or sidewalk approach to a bridge and commonly applied to a rather steep incline.

Random Stone. A general term applied to quarried stone block of any dimensions whether intended for ashlar or for random masonry construction.

Range of Stress. The algebraic difference between the minimum and maximum stresses in a member or in an element or part thereof either computed to be produced by a given condition of loading or produced by its actual service loading.

Rebar. A steel reinforcing bar.

Redundant Member. A member in a truss or frame which renders it a statistically indeterminate structure. The structure would be stable without the redundant member whose primary purpose is to reduce the stresses carried by the determinate structure.

Re-Entrant Corner. A corner with more than 180° of material and less than 180° of open space.

Reinforcing Bar. A steel bar, plain or with a deformed surface, which bonds to the concrete and supplies tensile strength to the concrete.

Retaining Wall. A structure designed to restrain and hold back a mass of earth.

Buttressed Wall. A retaining wall designed with projecting buttresses to provide strength and stability.

Counterforted Wall. A retaining wall designed with projecting counterforts to provide strength and stability.

Gravity Wall. A wall composed of brick, stone or concrete masonry designed to be stable against sliding and rotation (overturning) upon its foundation or upon any horizontal plane within its body by virtue of its shape and weight.

Reinforced Concrete Cantilever Wall. A wall consisting of a base section integral with stem constructed approximately at a right angle thereto giving its cross section a letter "L" or an inverted "T" shape. The stem portion resists the horizontal or other forces tending to produce overturning by acting as a cantilever beam.

Rigid Frame Bridge. A bridge with rigid or moment resistant connections between deck slabs or beams and the substructure walls or columns, producing an integral, elastic structure. The structure may be steel or concrete.

In general this type of bridge may be regarded as a form of arch or curved beam having its intermediate intradosal section or portion either straight or slightly curved and its end sections located normal to the straight portion or to the tangent of the curved one at its center length position.

Rim Girder. See DRUM GIRDER.

Rim Plate. Toothed or plain segmental rim on a rolling lift bridge.

Ringbolt. See EYEBOLT.

Ring Stone. See VOUSSOIR.

Riprap. Brickbats, stones, blocks of concrete or other protective covering material of like nature deposited upon river and stream beds and banks, lake, tidal or other shores to prevent erosion and scour by water flow, wave or other movement.

Rise of an Arch. For a symmetrical arch; the vertical distance from the chord through its springing lines to the intrados at its crown.

For an unsymmetrical arch, assumed to be in a normal vertical position, the vertical distances from its springing lines to the intrados at its crown.

Riveted Joint. (Bolted Joint.) A joint in which the assembled elements and members are united by rivets. The design of a riveted joint contemplates a proper distribution of its rivets to develop its various parts with relation to the stresses and the purposes which each must serve.

A bolted joint differs from a riveted one only in the use of bolts as the uniting medium instead of rivets. The conditions of design are generally the same, but different allowable unit stresses are employed.

Roadway. (*Travel Way.*) 1. The portion of the deck surface of a bridge intended for the use of vehicular or vehicular and pedestrian traffic. 2. The top surface portion of an approach embankment, causeway or cut intended for the general use of vehicular or vehicular and pedestrian traffic. In general, its width corresponds (1) to the distance curb to curb; (2) to the distance between the outside limits of sidewalks; or (3) to the width of the roadway pavement or traveled way when no curbs exist.

Roadway Shoulder Area. (*Shoulder Area.*) The portion or area of the top surface of an approach embankment, causeway, or cut immediately adjoining the roadway, used to accommodate stopped vehicles in emergencies and to laterally support base and surface courses.

Rocker Bearing. A cylindrical, sector-shaped member attached by a pin or trunnion at its axis location to the expansion end of a girder or truss and having line bearing contact upon its perimetral surface with the masonry plate or pedestal, thus providing for the longitudinal movements resulting from temperature changes and superimposed loads by a wheel-like translation.

The design condition that the entire reaction stress is concentrated upon a line contact renders it especially essential that the masonry plate or pedestal be accurately leveled and that the rocker be carefully adjusted to secure a uniform even bearing thereon. A relatively large percentage of this type of bearings lack correct adjustment.

Rocker Bent. A bent composed of metal, reinforced concrete or timber, hinged or otherwise articulated at one or both ends to provide the longitudinal movements resulting from temperature changes and the superimposed loads of the span or spans supported thereon.

Rocker and Camshaft. An adjustable bearing device or assemblage consisting of a rocker bearing combined with a camshaft, properly mounted and geared to produce by its rotation a vertical lifting action, reacting upon a shoe plate or pedestal fixed upon the bridge seat. When installed at each outermost end of the girders, or the trusses of a swing span, the lifting action raises them to an extent that their camber or droop will be removed and the areas rendered free to act as simple spans. When the camshafts are revolved through an angle of 180° from their total or full lift position the rocker bearings are released and lifted and the span is free to be moved to "open" position.

Rolled Beams, Rolled Shapes. See STRUCTURAL SHAPES, WIDE FLANGE BEAMS.

Roller. 1. A steel cylinder forming an element of a roller nest or any other device or part intended to provide movements by rolling contact. The so-termed "segmental roller" consisting essentially of two circular segments integrally joined by a web-like portion is used in the construction of roller nests requiring relatively large bearing length with the least practicable shoe plate area and a correspondingly decreased weight of metal in the entire assemblage. 2. One of the wheel-like elements forming the roller circle of a rim-bearing swing span.

Roller Bearing. A single roller or a group of rollers so housed as to permit movement of a part or parts of a structure thereon.

Roller Nest. A group of steel cylinders forming a part of the movable end of a girder or truss and located between the masonry plate and shoe or pedestal to facilitate the longitudinal movements resulting from temperature changes and superimposed loads. Commonly the rollers are assembled in a frame or a box. Roller nests may be used for other services than those herein described. The term "Expansion Rollers" is sometimes used synonymously for roller nest.

Roller Track. The circular track upon which the drum rollers of a rim-bearing swing span travel. This is sometimes described as the lower track.

Roller Tread. See TREAD PLATES.

Rolling Lift Bridge. See MOVABLE BRIDGE.

Rubble. Irregularly shaped pieces of stone in the undressed condition obtained from the quarry and commonly ranging in size from relatively small usable pieces to one-man or two-man stones. This term is also applied to large boulders and fragments requiring mechanical equipment for handling. When shaped ready for use in rubble masonry, this stone is commonly described as "worked" or "dressed" rubble.

Run-Off. As applied to bridge design, the portion of the precipitation upon a drainage (catchment) area which is discharged quickly by its drainage stream or streams and which, therefore, becomes a factor in the design of the effective water discharge area of a bridge. Run-off is dependent upon soil porosity (varied by saturated or frozen condition), slope or soil surfaces, intensity of rainfall or of melting snow conditions, and other pertinent factors.

S

Saddle. A member located upon the topmost portion of the tower of a suspension bridge, designed to support the suspension cable or chain and to provide for its horizontal movements resulting from elastic deformations induced by temperature changes and the stresses incident to the service loadings.

Safe Load. The maximum loading determined by a consideration of its magnitudes and distributions of wheel, axle or other concentrations as productive of unit stresses in the various members and incidental details of a structure, permissible for service use, due consideration being given to the physical condition of the structure resulting from its previous service use.

Safety Curb. A narrow curb between 9 inches and 24 inches wide serving as a refuge or walkway for pedestrians crossing a bridge.

Sag. A deformation of an entire span; of any part of a span, or of one or more of its members from the horizontal, vertical, or inclined position intended as a condition of its original design and construction. This variation may result from elastic deformation of structural material; from irregularities produced by inadequate temporary supports during the progress of construction operations; or from incorrect adjustments and unworkmanlike procedures made a part of the work.

In existing structures sag may be attributable to (1) original construction irregularities; (2) to excessive stresses resulting from overloading; (3) to corrosion, decay or other deterioration of the structure materials, and (4) plastic flow of material.

The total deflection of the cable members of a suspension bridge. The so-termed "sag ratio" is the relation existing between the sag and the length of span.

Sag Rod. A rod usually fitted with threads and nuts at its ends; used to restrain a structure member from sagging due to its own weight or to external force or forces.

Sash Brace. (*Sash Stay, Sash Strut.*) A horizontal or nearly horizontal piece bolted or otherwise secured upon the side of a pile or framed bent between the cap and ground surface or the cap and sill, as the case may be, thus adding rigidity to the assemblage.

The horizontal member in a tier of bracing attached to a timber, reinforced concrete, or metal trestle bent or tower.

Scab. (*Scab Piece.*) A plank spiked or bolted over the joint between two members to hold them in correct adjustment and strengthen the joint.

A short piece of I-beam or other structural shape bolted, riveted or welded upon the flange and/or web of a metal pile to increase its resistance to penetration. Similarly, for the same purpose, a piece of dense hardwood fitted upon the flange and/or web and having bearing upon a lug angle at one or both its ends.

Scour. An erosion of a river, stream, tidal inlet, lake or other water bed area by a current, wash or other water in motion, producing a deepening of the overlying water, or a widening of the lateral dimension of the flow area.

Screw Jack and Pedestal. An adjustable device or assemblage consisting of a screw operated within a fixed nut and having upon its bottom end a pedestal-like bearing conjoined with it by a ball and socket or other equally adaptable articulation permitting its adjustment upon a shoe plate or pedestal fixed upon the bridge seat. When installed at each outermost end of the girders or the trusses of a swing span their major function is to lift them to an extent that their camber or droop will be removed and the arms rendered free to act as simple spans.

Scupper. (*Curb Inlet.*) An opening in the floor portion of a bridge, commonly located adjacent to the curb or wheel guard, to provide means for rain or other water accumulated upon the roadway surface to drain through it into the space beneath the structure. Bridges having reinforced concrete floors with concrete curbs may be effectively drained through scuppers located within the curb face surfaces.

Scupper Block. One of the short wooden pieces fixed between the wooden planks of a bridge floor and the bottom side of the wheel guard to provide open spaces beneath the latter for draining rain or other water accumulation from the floor surface.

Seam Weld. A weld joining the edges of two elements of a member or of two members placed in contact. This weld serves to form a continuous surface whether plane or curved, and to prevent infiltration of moisture between the parts. In general, it is not a stress carrying weld.

Seat Angle. (*Shelf Angle.*) A piece of angle attached upon the side of a column girder or other member to provide support for a connecting member either temporarily during its erection or permanently. The outstanding leg of the angle may be strengthened by a stiffener placed vertically beneath it.

Segmental Girder and Track Girder. These terms apply to the rolling lift type of bascule bridge combining circular rotation and translation movements in the "opening-closing" cycle.

The term "segmental girder" is used to designate one of the movable operating girders of a span or leaf to which a span girder or truss is rigidly attached. It commonly consists of a plate girder having its bottom flange curved to form a segment of a circle. This curved flange is fitted with tread castings which take line bearing contact upon the tread castings fitted upon the top flange of the supporting track girder with which they interlock to insure positive translation movement.

The term "track girder" is used to designate one of the plate girders or trusses intended to provide support for the movable span throughout an "opening-closing" cycle. Its tread castings fitted upon its top flange or chord form the track upon which the segmental girder moves by a rack and pinion-like action.

Segmental Rim. The curved rim or circular segment of a rolling lift bridge.

Seizing. The ligature of wire or other material applied upon a suspension bridge cable to hold the individual wires in satisfactory contact condition.

Separator. See SPREADER.

Shafts. Pieces conveying torsion stress only, which are, in general, used only in movable structures.

Shear Lock. (*Heel Stay, Tail-Lock.*) The device or mechanism provided at the heel of a bascule span to engage and hold the leaf in its closed position and prevent rotation.

Sheave. A wheel having a groove or grooves in its face surface. This term may be applied collectively to include both the sheave and its housing block.

Sheave Girder. A girder or girder-like member supporting the operating cable sheaves at the top of a tower of a vertical lift bridge.

Sheave Hood. A protecting covering placed above a sheave engaging the suspending cables of a vertical lift bridge to prevent accumulations of moisture, sleet and ice upon the sheave face.

Sheet Pile Cofferdam. In general a wall-like, watertight or nearly watertight barrier composed of driven timber or metal sheet piling constructed to surround the area to be occupied by an abutment, pier, retaining wall or other structure and permit unwatering of the enclosure so that the excavation for the preparation of a foundation and the abutment, pier or other construction may be produced in the open air. The alignment of the piles may be facilitated by the use of walers, struts and ties.

This type of dam is adapted to construction located in still or slow flowing shallow water. Its watertightness is sometimes rendered more complete by depositing earth material against the exterior side of the dam.

Sheet Piling. (*Sheeting.*) A general or collective term used to describe a number of sheet piles taken together to form a crib, cofferdam, bulkhead, etc.

Shelf Angle. See SEAT ANGLE.

Shim. A comparatively thin piece of wood, stone, or metal inserted between two elements, pieces or members to fix their relative position and/or to transmit bearing stress.

Shoe. In general, a pedestal-shaped member at the end of a plate girder or truss functioning to transmit and distribute its loads to a masonry bearing area or to any other supporting area or member. A shoe may be a cast or a built-up member; the base plate or plate-like part of which is commonly termed the "shoe plate," which may take bearing directly upon a masonry plate or upon an intervening expansion device.

Shore. A strut or prop placed in a horizontal, inclined or vertical position against or beneath a structure or a portion thereof to restrain movement.

Shoulder Area. See ROADWAY SHOULDER AREA.

Sidewalk. The portion of the bridge floor area serving pedestrian traffic only and, for safety and convenience to its users, commonly elevated above the portion occupied by vehicles.

Sidewalk Bracket. As applied to metal structures: A trianguar shaped frame attached to and projecting from the outside of a girder, truss or bent to serve as a support for the sidewalk stringers, floor and railing or parapet. In general, these brackets are in effect a cantilevered extension of the floor beams and are commonly connected to them by bars or other tension pieces designed to sustain the bending moment at the junction plane.

As applied to reinforced concrete structures: A cantilever beam commonly triangular in shape, attached to and projecting from the outside of a girder, truss, or bent to serve as a support for the sidewalk floor slab and the railing or parapet.

Sill. (*Sill Piece.*) The base piece or member of a viaduct or trestle bent serving to distribute the column loads directly upon the foundation or upon mud sills embedded in the foundation soil transversely to the alignment of the bent.

Silt. Very finely divided siliceous or other hard and durable rock material derived from its mother rock through attritive or other mechanical action rather than chemical decomposition. In general, its grain size shall be that which will pass a Standard No. 200 sieve.

Simple Span. A superstructure span having, at each end, a single unrestraining bearing or support and designed to be unaffected by stress transmission to or from an adjacent span or structure.

S-I-P Forms. See FORMS.

Skew Angle. As applied to oblique bridges; the skew angle, angle of skew or simply "skew" is the acute angle subtended by a line normal to the longitudinal axis of the structure and a line parallel to or coinciding with the alignment of its end.

Skewback. The course of stones, in an abutment or pier, located at the extremity of an arch and having its beds inclined (battered) as required to transmit the stresses of the arch. The bed adjoining the voussoirs forming the first string course of the arch ring will be normal to the axis of the arch. The individual stones of the skewback course are designated "skewback stones."

A casting or a combination of castings; or a built-up member designed to function as a skewback.

Skewback Shoe. (*Skewback Pedestal.*) The shoe or pedestal member, transmitting the thrust of a trussed arch or a plate girder arch to the skewback course or cushion course of an abutment or pier. Skewback shoes and pedestals are commonly hinged.

Slab. A thick plate, usually of reinforced concrete, which supports load by flexure. It is usually treated as a widened beam.

Slab Bridge. A bridge having a superstructure composed of a reinforced concrete slab constructed either as a single unit or as a series of narrow slabs placed parallel with the roadway alignment and spanning the space between the supporting abutments or other substructure parts. The former is commonly constructed in place but the latter may be precast.

Slag Inclusion. Small particles of slag trapped inside a weld during the fusion process.

Sleeve Nut. A device used to connect the elements of an adjustable rod or bar member. It consists of a forging having an elongated nut-shaped body with right- and left-hand threads within its end portions, thus permitting its adjustment with a wrench to provide a desired tension in the member.

Slenderness Ratio. Measure of stiffness of a member, expressed as the length of the member divided by its radius of gyration.

Slope. A term commonly applied to the inclined surface of an excavated cut or an embankment.

Slope Pavement. (*Slope Protection.*) A thin surfacing of stone, concrete or other material deposited upon the sloped surface of an approach cut, embankment or causeway to prevent its disintegration by rain, wind or other erosive action.

Slot Weld. See PLUG WELD.

Soffit. See INTRADOS.

Sole Plate. A plate bolted, riveted, or welded upon the bottom flange of a rolled beam, plate girder, or truss to take direct bearing upon a roller nest, bearing pedestal, or masonry plate. It distributes the reaction of the bearing to the beam, girder, or truss member. The sole plate may also function as a combined sole and masonry plate at the fixed end of a beam, girder, or truss.

Soldier Beam. A steel pile driven into the earth with its butt end projecting, used as a cantilever beam to support horizontal lagging retaining an excavated surface.

Spalls. Circular or oval depression in concrete caused by a separation of a portion of the surface concrete, revealing a fracture parallel with or slightly inclined to the surface. Usually part of the rim is perpendicular to the surface.

The pieces of spalled concrete themselves.

Span. This term has various applications depending upon its use whether in design, in field construction, or in its common nontechnical application, viz.:

When applied to design of a beam, girder, truss or arch structure. The distance center to center of the end bearings or the distance between the lines of action of the reactions whether induced by substructure or other supporting members.

When applied to the field construction of substructure abutments and piers. The unobstructed space or distance between the faces of the substructure elements. For arch structures this length is measured at the elevation of the springing lines. These lengths or dimensions are commonly referred to as "clear span length." See CLEAR SPAN.

The complete superstructure of a single span bridge or a corresponding integral part or unit of a multiple span structure. This application of "span" is rendered more specific when subdivided into: (a) **Fixed Span**: A superstructure anchored in its location upon the substructure and (b) **Movable Span**: A superstructure intended to be swung or lifted to provide an unobstructed waterway space for the passage of waterborne traffic.

Spandrel. The space bounded by the arch extrados, the substructure abutments and/or pier(s), and the roadway surface or other elevation limit fixed by the construction details.

Spandrel Column. A column superimposed upon the ring or a rib of an arch span and serving as a support for the deck construction of an open spandrel arch. See OPEN SPANDREL ARCH.

Spandrel Fill. The filling material placed within the spandrel space of a spandrel arch.

Spandrel Tie. A wall or a beam-like member connecting the spandrel walls of an arch and securing them against bulging and other deformation. In stone masonry arches the spandrel tie walls served to some extent as counterforts. In reinforced concrete spandrel arch spans spandrel tie walls may likewise serve as counterforts. See TIE WALLS.

Spandrel Wall. A wall built upon an arch to function as a retaining wall for the spandrel fill and the roadway in a spandrel filled structure; but, when the spandrel is not filled, to support the floor system and its loads. In wide structures having unfilled spandrels one or more interior walls may be used, thus providing a cellular construction when combined with tie walls. See TIE WALLS.

Specifications. A detailed enumeration of the chemical and physical properties determining the quality of construction materials together with requirements for handling, shipping and storage thereof; the conditions governing the loads, load applications and unit stress considerations of bridge foundation, substructure and superstructure design; the development of construction details and their applications incident to fabrication; erecton or other construcon procedures pertinent to the production of serviceable bridge structures.

When general or so called "standard" specifications are used, it occasionally becomes necessary to supplement the requirements by items having specific application to a given bridge structure or group of structures. The special items may either designate and authorize departures from the "standard" or apply entirely to requirements and conditions not dealt with therein. The status of these supplemental or special specifications is commonly fixed by the "standard" specifications. Likewise the "standard" specification commonly recognizes the possibility of discrepancies between the specifications and the general plans and working (detail) drawings by fixing a coordination status for such occurrences.

Spider. The collar-like plate connecting the spider frame of a rim bearing or a combined rim and center bearing swing span to the pivot.

Spider Frame. The frame assemblage of struts, radial rods, spacer rings and roller adjusting devices holding the conical roller ring of a rim bearing or a combined rim and center bearing swing span in correct position with relation to the pivot.

Spider Rod. See RADIAL ROD.

Splay Saddle. A member at the anchorage ends of suspension bridge cables which permits the wires or strands to spread so that they may be connected to the anchorage.

Splice. This term has two applications depending upon its use whether in design or in shop and field construction, viz.:

When applied to design and the development of construction details: The joining or uniting of elements of a member, parts of a member or members of a structure to provide desired conditions for the transmittal of stress and the development of rigidity and general strength fulfilling the service requirements of the member or of the structure of which it is a part.

When applied to shop and field construction: the complete assemblage of parts used in producing the union of elements of a member or members of a structure.

Splice Joint. A joint in which the elements of a member or the members of a structure are joined by a splice plate or by a part or piece functioning to secure a required amount of strength and stability.

Spreader. 1. A cast or fabricated piece used to hold angles, beams, channels or fabricated pieces or parts in the locations or positions in which they function as parts of a member or structure. 2. A ring-like or sleeve-like piece placed upon a pin to hold the eyebars or other members assembled upon it in their correct member positions. This piece is sometimes described as a "pin-filler," or "packing ring."

Springing Line. The line within the face surface of an abutment or pier at which the intrados of an arch takes its beginning or origin.

Starling. An extension at the upstream end only, or at both the upstream and downstream ends of a pier built with surfaces battered thus forming a cutwater to divide and deflect the stream waters and floating debris and, correspondingly, when on the downstream end, functioning to reduce crosscurrents, swirl and eddy action which are productive of depositions of sand, silt and detritus downstream from the pier.

Statics. The branch of physical science which is concerned with bodies acted on by balanced forces. Therefore, these bodies are either at rest or static.

Stay-In-Place Forms. See FORMS.

Stay Plate. (*Tie Plate.*) A plate placed at or near the end of a latticed side or web of a compression or other member and also at intermediate locations where connections for members interrupt the continuity of the latticing. This plate serves to distribute the lattice bar stress to the elements of the member and adds stiffness and rigidity to joint assemblages.

Stem. The vertical wall portion of an abutment retaining wall, or solid pier. See also BREASTWALL.

Stiffener. An angle, tee, plate or other rolled section riveted, bolted or welded upon the web of a plate girder or other "built-up" member to transfer stress and to prevent buckling or other deformation.

A stiffener forged at its ends to fit upon the web and the web-legs of the flange angles of a plate girder is termed "crimped."

Stiffening Girder, Stiffening Truss. A girder or truss incorporated in a suspension bridge to function in conjunction with a suspension cable or chain by restraining the deformations of the latter and by distributing the concentrated or other irregularly distributed loads thus resisting and controlling the vertical oscillations of the floor system imparted to it by the cable or chain deformations.

Stirrup. In timber and metal bridges: A U-shaped rod, bar or angle piece providing a stirrup-like support for an element of a member or a member.

In reinforced concrete bridges: A U-shaped bar placed in beams, slabs or similar constructions to resist diagonal tension stresses.

Stirrup Bolt. A U-shaped rod or bar fitted at its ends with threads, nuts and washers and used to support streamer or other timber pieces of wooden truss structures suspended from the bottom chord.

Stone Facing. (*Stone Veneer, Brick Veneer.*) A stone or brick surface covering or sheath laid in imitation of stone or brick masonry but having a depth thickness equal to the width dimension of one stone or brick for stretchers and the length dimension for headers. The backing portion of a wall or the interior portion of a pier may be constructed of rough stones imbedded in mortar or concrete, cyclopean concrete, plain or reinforced concrete, brick bats imbedded in mortar, or even of mortar alone. The backing and interior material may be deposited as the laying of the facing material progresses to secure interlocking and bonding with it, or the covering material may be laid upon its preformed surface.

Strain. The distortion of a body produced by the application of one or more external forces and measured in units of length. In common usage, this is the proportional relation of the amount of distortion divided by the original length.

Stress. The resistance of a body tp distortion when in a solid or plastic state and when acting in an unconfined condition. Stress is produced by the strain (distortion) and holds in equilibrium the external forces causing the distortion. It is measured in pounds or tons. Within the elastic limit the strain in a member of a structure is proportional to the stress in that member.

Allowable Unit Stress. As applied to the investigation of an existing structure in determining its adequacy for existing or prospective service; it is the stress per unit of area of the material of the entire structure or any portion or member thereof which is determined to be a safe unit for service use, due consideration being given to the quality of the material, physical condition, the adequacy of the construction details or other physical factors incident or pertinent to the service conditions to which they are or will be subjected and, if necessary, to the conditions contemplated to exist in the event of repair, replacement or strengthening operations.

Unit Stress. The stress per square inch (or other unit of surface or crosssectional area). The Allowable Unit Stress is: (a) Assumed in determining the composition and construction details of a memer or the members of a proposed structure, or (b) assumed for judging the safe load-capacity of an existing structure; while working stress is (c) produced in the members and parts of an existing structure when subjected to loads, impacts and other stress-producing elements and factors to which the structure is proposed to be or may have been subjected.

Working Stress. The unit stress in a member under service or design load.

Stress Sheet. A drawing showing a structure in skeletal form sufficient only to impart or suggest in conjunction with notations thereon its general makeup, major dimensions and the arrangement and composition of its integral parts. Special construction details may be shown by section views and sketches with or without dimensional data. Upon the skeletal outline of the structure or in tabulated form the drawing should show the computed stresses resulting from the application of a system of loads together with the design composition of the individual members resulting from the application of assumed unit stresses for the material or materials to be used in the structures. The assumed design load or loads should appear either in diagrammatic form with dimensions and magnitudes, or reference be made to readily available information relating thereto by a special note conspicuously displayed upon the drawing. A future investigation of a given structure to determine its reliability for a given load or combination of loads may be greatly facilitated and expedited by an adequate stress sheet record of its original design conditions.

Stringer. A longitudinal beam supporting the bridge deck, and in large bridges or truss bridges, framed into or upon the floor beams.

Structural Members. Basically these are of three types, viz.: (1) Ties: Pieces subject to axial tension only; (2) Columns or Struts: Pieces subject to axial compression only; (3) Beams: Pieces transversely loaded and subject to both shear and bending moment.

However, the arrangement of the members of a structure and the application of its design loads may embody combinations of these basic stress types.

Structural Shapes. As applied to bridge structures: The various types and forms of rolled iron and steel having flat, round, angle, channel, "I", "H", "Z" and other cross-sectional shapes adapted to the construction of the metal members incorporated in reinforced foundations, substructures and superstructures.

Structural Tee. A tee-shaped rolled member formed by cutting a wide flange longitudinally along the centerline of web.

Strut. A general term applying to a piece or member acting to resist compressive stress.

Sub-Panel. See PANEL.

Subpunched and Reamed Work. A term applied to structural steel shapes having rivet holes punched a specified dimension less in diameter than the nominal size of the rivets to be driven therein and subsequently reamed to a specified diameter greater than the rivet size.

This term is also applied to completely assembled and riveted members and structures in which the rivet holes have been produced by subpunching and reaming procedure.

Substructure. The abutments, piers, grillage or other constructions built to support the span or spans of a bridge superstructure whether consisting of beam, girder, truss, trestle or other type or types of construction.

Sump. A pit or tank-like depression or receptacle into which water is drained. The removal of the water so accumulated may be effected by pumping or by siphoning.

Superelevation. (*Curve Banking.*) The transverse inclination of the roadway surface within a horizontal curve and the relatively short tangent lengths adjacent thereto required for its full development. The purpose of superelevation is to provide a means of resisting or overcoming the centrifugal forces of vehicles in transit.

Superstructure. The entire portion of a bridge structure which primarily receives and supports highway, railway, canal, or other traffic loads and in its turn transfers the reactions resulting therefrom to the bridge substructure. The superstructure may consist of beam, girder, truss, trestle or other type or types of construction.

A superstructure may consist of a single span upon two supports or of a combination of two or more spans having the number and distribution of supports required by their types of construction, whether consisting of simple, continuous, cantilever, suspension, arch or trestle span-tower-bent construction.

Surcharge. An additional load placed atop existing earth or dead loads. In the case of abutments and retaining walls, the surcharge load is assumed to be replaced by an earth load of equivalent total weight.

Suspended Span. A superstructure span having one or both of its ends supported upon or from adjoining cantilever arms, brackets or towers, and designed to be unaffected by other stress transmission to or from an adjacent structure. The ordinary use of a suspended span is in connection with cantilever span construction.

Suspender. A wire cable, a metal rod or bar designed to engage a cable band or other device connecting it to the main suspension member of a suspension bridge at one end and a member of the bridge floor system at the other thus permitting it to assist in supporting the bridge floor system and its superimposed loads by transferring loads to the main suspension members of the structure.

A member serving to support another member in a horizontal or an inclined position against sagging, twisting or other deformation due to its own weight.

Suspension Bridge. A bridge in which the floor system and its incidental parts and appliances are supported in practically a horizontal position by being suspended upon cables which are supported at two or more locations upon towers and are anchored at their extreme ends. The cables constitute the main suspension members and commonly their anchorage may be one of three forms, viz.: (1) By extension of these members beyond the towers to the anchorages; (2) By fixing their ends upon the towers and backstaying the towers against overturning by the suspension members pulling upon them; (3) By an integral inclusion of the anchorages within the structure whereby the entire horizontal and vertical components of the main suspension member stresses are resisted by a rigid floor system construction functioning as a column, upon the extreme ends of which the main suspension members are securely connected. This form is commonly described as "self anchored."

Suspension Cable. (*Suspension Chain.*) One of the main members upon which the floor system of a suspension bridge is supported. Its ends may be fixed at the tops of towers which are backstayed to resist the horizontal components of the cable or chain stresses or instead it may rest upon saddles at the tops of two or more towers and be extended and fixed upon anchorage members. When the extension portions from the tops of towers to the anchorages do not directly support any part of the bridge floor, they function essentially as backstays; but when they engage floor suspenders located between the towers and anchorages they function as suspension cables for the end spans of the structure.

Sway Anchorage. (*Sway Cable.*) A guy, stay cable or chain attached at an intermediate length location upon the floor system of a suspension bridge and anchored upon the end portion of an abutment or pier or in the adjacent land surface to increase the resistance of the suspension span to lateral movement.

Sway Brace. 1. A piece bolted, or otherwise secured in an inclined position upon the side of a pile or frame bent between the cap and ground surface or the cap and sills, as the case may be, to add rigidity to the assemblage. See BRAC-

ING. 2. An inclined member in a tier of bracing forming a part of a timber, metal, or R/C bent or tower. 3. One of the inclined members of the sway bracing system of a metal girder or truss span. In plate girder construction the term X-brace is sometimes used.

Sway Frame. A complete panel or frame of sway bracing. See BRACING.

Swedge Bolt. See ANCHOR BOLT.

Swing Span. A superstructure span designed to be entirely supported upon a pier at its center, when its end supports have been withdrawn or released, and equipped to be revolved in a horizontal plane to free a navigable waterway of the obstruction it presents to navigation when in its normal traffic service position. See MOVABLE BRIDGE.

Swing Span Pivot. The center casting upon or about which the movable portion of a swing span revolves in making an opening-closing cycle.

In the center bearing type span, this casting functions not only as a pivotal member but also as the support for the movable span when the end lifting device is released.

In the rim-bearing type span this casting functions as a pivotal anchor member regulating the location of the movable parts throughout an opening-closing cycle but does not support the movable span.

In the combined center and rim-bearing type this casting functions as a support for a portion of the weight of the movable span when the end lifting device is released.

T

Tack Weld. A weld of the butt, fillet or seam type intended only to fix an element of a member or a member of a structure in correct adjustment and position preparatory to fully welding. Tack welds may be used to restrain welded parts against deformation and distortion resulting from expansion of the metal by atmospheric and welding temperatures.

Tail Lock. See SHEAR LOCK.

Tail Pit. See COUNTERWEIGHT WELL.

Tail Water. Water ponded below the outlet of a culvert, pipe, or bridge waterway, thereby reducing the amount of flow through the waterway. Tailwater is expressed in terms of its depth. See also HEADWATER.

Temporary Bridge. A structure built for emergency or interim use to replace a previously existing bridge demolished or rendered unserviceable by flood, fire, wind or other untoward occurrence, or instead, to supply bridge service required for a relatively short period.

Tendon. A prestressing cable or strand.

Tension. An axial force or stress caused by equal and opposite forces pulling at the ends of the members.

Throat. Of a fillet weld. The dimension normal to the sloping face of a fillet weld between the heel of the weld and the sloping faces.

Through Bridge. A bridge having its floor elevation more nearly at the elevation of the bottom than at the top portion of the superstructure, thus providing for the passage of traffic between the supporting parts.

Tide Gate. See FLOOD GATE.

Tie Plate. See STAY PLATE.

Tie Rod. (*Tie Bar*.) A rod-like or bar-like member in a truss or other frame functioning to transmit tensile stress.

Tie Walls. (*Spandrel Tie Wall*.) One of the walls built at intervals above the arch ring to tie together and reinforce the spandrel walls. See DIAPHRAGM WALL.

Any wall designed to serve as a restraining member to prevent bulging and distortion of two other walls connected thereby.

Toe of Slope. The location defined by the intersection of the sloped surface of an approach cut, embankment or causeway or other sloped area with the natural or an artifical ground surface existing at a lower elevation.

Toe Wall. (*Footwall*.) A relatively low retaining wall placed near the "toe-of-slope" location of an approach embankment or causeway to produce a fixed termination or to serve as a protection against erosion and scour or, perhaps, to prevent the accumulation of stream debris.

Toggle Joint. A mechanical arrangement wherein two members are hinged together, in fact or in effect, at a central location and hinged separately at their opposite ends; their alignment forming an obtuse angle so that a force applied at the common hinge location will produce a thrust acting at the end hinges, laterally to the alignment or direction of the original force.

Tolerance. (*Margin.*) A range or variation in physical or chemical properties specified or otherwise determined as permissible for the acceptance and use of construction materials.

Tower. 1. A three dimension substructure framework in a viaduct type structure having the vertical bents at its ends joined longitudinally by struts and braces thus rendering the assemblage so formed effective in resisting forces acting longitudinally upon the structure. 2. A four-sided frame supporting the ends of two spans or instead one complete span (tower span) and the ends of two adjacent spans of a viaduct; having its column members strutted and braced in tiers and the planes of either two or four sides battered. 3. A pier or a frame serving to support the cables or chains of a suspension type bridge at the end of a span. 4. A frame functioning as an end support, guide frame and counterweight support for a vertical lift span during an operating cycle.

Track Girder. See SEGMENTAL GIRDER.

Track Plate. The plate, toothed or plain, upon which the segmental girder of a rolling lift span rolls.

Track Segment. One of the assemblage pieces of the circular track supporting the balance wheels of a center bearing swing span or the drum bearing wheels of a drum or combined center and drum bearing span.

Transition Length. The tangent length within which the change from a normal to a superelevated roadway cross section is developed.

Transverse Bracing. (*Transverse System.*) The bracing assemblage engaging the columns of trestle and viaduct bents and towers in perpendicular or slightly inclined planes and in the horizontal or nearly horizontal planes of their sash braces to function in resisting the transverse forces resulting from wind, lateral vibration and traffic movements tending to produce lateral movement and deformation of the columns united thereby. See BRACING.

Transverse Girder. See CROSS GIRDER.

Travel Way. See ROADWAY.

Tread Plates. (*Roller Tread.*) The plates attached upon the bottom flange of the drum girder; shaped to form a circular surface taking a uniform even bearing upon the drum rollers and thereby transferring to them the live and dead loads of the superimposed structure. The assemblage of tread plates is sometimes described as the "Upper Track."

Tremie. A long trunk or pipe used to place concrete under water. A tremie usually has a hopper at its upper end.

The concrete placed under water by use of a tremie is often called tremie concrete. In placing tremie concrete, it is important that the mouth of the tremie be kept immersed within the mass of concrete already deposited to prevent the water from mixing with the concrete, thereby weakening or destroying it.

Trestle. A bridge structure consisting of beam, girder or truss spans supported upon bents. The bents may be of the piled or of the frame type, composed of timber, reinforced concrete or metal. When of framed timbers, metal or reinforced concrete they may involve two or more tiers in their construction. Trestle structures are designated as "wooden," "frame," or "framed," "metal," "concrete," "wooden pile," "concrete pile," etc., depending upon or corresponding to the material and characteristics of their principal members.

Trailing Wheel. See BALANCE WHEEL.

Triangular Truss. See WARREN TRUSS.

Trunnion. As applied to a bascule bridge. The assemblage consisting essentially of a pin fitted into a supporting bearing and forming a hinge or axle upon which the movable span swings during an opening-closing cycle.

Trunnion Girder. The girder supporting the trunnions on a bascule bridge.

Truss. A jointed structure having an open built web construction so arranged that the frame is divided into a series of triangular figures with its component straight members primarily stressed axially only. The triangle is the truss element and each type of truss used in bridge construction is an assemblage of triangles. The connecting pins are assumed to be frictionless.

Truss Bridge. A bridge having a truss for a superstructure: The ordinary single span rests upon two supports, one at each end, which may be abutments, piers, bents or towers, or combinations thereof. The superstructure span may be divided into three parts, viz.: (1) the trusses, (2) the floor system and (3) the bracing.

Truss Panel. See PANEL.

Trussed Beam. A beam reinforced by one or more rods upon its tension side attached at or near its ends and passing beneath a support at the midlength of the span producing in effect an inverted King post truss. The support, if a wooden block, is commonly termed a "saddle block" but, if a cast iron or structural steel member it is termed a "stanchion."

Tubular Truss. A truss whose chords and struts are composed of pipes or cylindrical tubes.

Tudor Arch. See GOTHIC ARCH.

Turnbuckle. A device used to connect the elements of adjustable rod and bar members. It consists of a forging having nut-like end portions right and left hand threaded and integrally connected by two bars upon its opposite sides thus providing an intervening open space through which a lever may be inserted to adjust the tension in the member.

Turning Pinion and Rack. The pinion to which the power to operate a swing span is applied and the circular rack fixed upon the pivot pier upon which the pinion travels to produce its rotation movement. When a swing span requires a very considerable amount of power to operate it, two operating pinions located at opposite sides of the circular rack or nearly so are commonly used to distribute the operating force upon the rack and its anchorage.

U

U-Bolt. A bar, either round or square, bent in the shape of the letter "U" and fitted with threads and nuts at its ends.

Underpass. See OVERPASS.

Uplift. A negative reaction or a force tending to lift a beam, truss, pile, or any other bridge element upwards.

V

Vertical-Lift Bridge. See MOVABLE BRIDGE.

Viaduct. A bridge structure consisting of beam, girder, truss, or arch span supported upon abutments with towers or alternate towers and bents or with a series of piers (cylindrical, dumbbell, rectangular or other types), or with any combination of these types of supporting parts.

In general, a viaduct is regarded as having greater height than a trestle. However, this notion is inconsistent with bridge engineering practice. A viaduct may be in all respects like a multiple span bridge.

Vierendeel Truss. A rigid frame consisting essentially of an assemblage of rectangles and trapezoids with no diagonal members. Its service in a bridge is the same as that assigned to a plate girder or a truss.

Voided Unit. A precast concrete deck unit containing cylindrical voids to reduce dead load.

Voussoir. (*Ring Stone.*) One of the truncated wedge shaped stones composing a ring course in a stone arch. The facing or head voussoirs are those placed at the terminations of a ring course.

W

Wale. (*Wale-Piece, Waler.*) A wooden or metal piece or an assemblage of pieces placed either inside or outside, or both inside and outside, the wall portion of a crib, cofferdam or similar structure, usually in a horizontal position to maintain its shape and increase its rigidity, stability, and strength. An assemblage of wale pieces is termed a "waling," or "strake o' wail."

Warren Truss. (*Triangular Truss.*) A parallel chord truss developed for use in metal bridge structures, wherein the web system is usually formed by a single triangulation of members at an angle to each other. There are no counters but web members near the center of a span may be subject to stress reversals and are to be designed accordingly. Verticals may or may not be used.

Washer. A small metal disc having a hole in its center to engage a bolt or a rivet. It may be used beneath the nut or the head of a bolt or as a separator between elements of a member or the members of a structure.

Water Table. The upper limit or elevation of ground water saturating a portion of a soil mass.

Waterway. The available width for the passage of stream, tidal or other water beneath a bridge, if unobstructed by natural formations or by artificial constructions beneath or closely adjacent to the structure. For a multiple span bridge the available width is the total of the unobstructed waterway lengths of the spans. See CLEAR SPAN.

Wearing Surface. (*Wearing Course.*) The surface portion of a roadway area which is in direct contact with the means of transport and is, therefore, primarily subject to the abrading, crushing or other disintegrating effect produced by hammering, rolling, sliding or other physical action tending to induce attrition thereof.

A topmost layer or course of material applied upon a roadway to receive the traffic service loads and to resist the abrading, crushing or other distintegrating action resulting therefrom.

Web. The portion of a beam, girder or truss, located between and connected to the flanges or the chords. It serves mainly to resist shear stresses. The stem of a dumbbell or solid wall type pier.

Web Members. The intermediate members of a truss extending, in general, from chord to chord but not including the end posts. Inclined web members are termed diagonals. A "tie" is a diagonal in tension while a brace or strut is a diagonal in compression. A vertical web member in compression is commonly designated a post, while one in tension due entirely to the external forces applied at its lower end, is designated a hanger. The joint formed by the intersection of an inclined end post with the top chord is commonly designated the hip joint or "the hip" end and the vertical tension member engaging the hip joint is commonly known as the hip vertical or the first panel hanger.

Web Plate. The plate forming the web element of a plate girder, built-up beam or column.

Wedge and Pedestals. An adjustable bearing device or assemblage consisting of a wedge operating between an upper and a lower bearing block or pedestal, and when installed at each outermost end of the girders or the trusses of a swing span, functioning to lift them to an extent that their camber or "droop" will be removed and the arms rendered free to act as simple spans. Furthermore, when installed beneath the loading girder of a center bearing swing span they serve to relieve the pivot bearing from all or nearly all live load and to stabilize the center portion of the span. When the wedges are withdrawn and the end latching device released, the span is free to be moved to an "open" position.

Lifting devices of the wedge and pedestal type may be used under the loading girder of a center bearing swing span in conjunction with rocker and eccentric, link and roller, or other end lifting devices at the ends of the span.

However, some swing spans of short length and placed in rather unimportant locations are designed to support both dead and live loads upon the center pivot and the ends of span are inadequately lifted with the result that they "end hammer" upon their pedestals.

Wedge Stroke. The theoretical travel distance a wedge must move upon its pedestal to lift the end of the arm of a swing span a distance equal to the vertical camber or "droop" of the arm due to elastic deformation minus the portion assumed to be provided in the field erection operation.

The actual elastic deformation of the arms of a given swing span may vary considerably from the theoretical due probably to temperature variations during the periods in which fabrication and erection are in progress, or to variation in the friction developed between the elements combined to form joints and to other incidental irregularities.

Weep Hole. (*Weep Pipe.*) An open hole or an embedded pipe in a masonry retaining wall, abutment, arch or other portion of a masonry structure to provide means of drainage for the embankment, causeway, spandrel backfill or retained soil wherein water may accumulate.

Weld. The process of uniting portions of one or more pieces, the elements of a member, or the members of a structure in an intimate and permanent position or status by (1) the application of pressure induced by the blow of a hammer or by a pressure machine, the portions to be united having been previously heated to a so-called welding temperature and the junction areas cleaned and purified by the application of fluxing material, or by (2) the use of a high temperature flame to preheat the metal adjacent to the weld location and when it has attained a molten temperature to add molten weld metal, in conjunction with fluxing material, in sufficient quantity to produce a fully filled joint when cooled or by (3) the use of the electric arc to obtain a molten temperature in the metal closely adjacent to the weld location and to supply in the arc stream molten filler metal and fluxing material requisite to produce by coalescence of the structure and electrode metals a fully filled joint.

The joint produced by the application of a welding process.

Weld Layer. A single thickness of weld metal composed of beads (runs) laid in contact to form a pad weld or a portion of a weld made up of superimposed beads.

Weld Metal. The fused filler metal which is added to the fused structure metal to produce by coalescence and interdiffusion a welded joint or a weld layer.

Weld Penetration. The depth beneath the original surface, to which the structure metal has been fused in the making of a fusion weld. See PENETRATION.

Weld Sequence. The order of succession required for making the welds of a built-up piece or the joints of a structure to avoid, so far as practicable, the residual stresses producing or tending to produce individual joint distortions and deformations of the structure or its members.

Welded Bridge. (*Welded Structure.*) A structure wherein the metal elements composing its members and the joints whereby these members are combined into the structure frame, are united by welds.

Welded Joint. A joint in which the assembled elements and members are united through fusion of metal. The design of a welded joint contemplates a proper distribution of the welds to develop its various parts with relation to the stresses and the purpose which each must serve, due consideration being given to factors productive of secondary stresses through weld shrinkage, warping and other conditions attending weld fabrication.

Wheel Base. A term applied to the axle spacing or lengths of vehicles. When applied to automobiles and trucks having wheel concentrations at the ends of the front and rear axles it is the length center to center of axles or the longitudinal dimension center to center of front and rear wheels.

Wheel Concentration. (*Wheel Load.*) The load carried by and transmitted to the supporting structure by one wheel. This concentration may involve the wheel of a traffic vehicle, a movable bridge, or other motive equipment or device. See AXLE LOAD.

Wheel Guard. (*Filloe Guard.*) A timber piece placed longitudinally along the side limit of the roadway to guide the movements of vehicle wheels and safeguard the bridge trusses, railings and other constructions existing outside the roadway limit from collision with vehicles and their loads.

Whiteway Lighting. The lighting provided for nighttime illumination along a road or bridge, as distinguished from sign lighting or colored regulatory and warning lights.

Wide Flange. (*Carnegie Beam.*) A rolled member having an H-shaped cross section, differentiated from an I-beam in that the flanges are wider and the web thinner.

Wind Bracing. The bracing systems in girder and truss spans and in towers and bents which function to resist the stresses induced by wind forces.

Wing Wall. The retaining wall extension of an abutment intended to restrain and hold in place the side slope material of an approach causeway or embankment. When flared at an angle with the breast wall it serves also to deflect stream water and floating debris into the waterway of the bridge and thus protects the approach embankment against erosion. The general forms of wing walls are:

(1) Straight—in continuation of the breast wall of the abutment.

(2) U-type—placed parallel to the alignment of the approach roadway.

(3) Flared—forming an angle with the alignment of the abutment breast wall by receding therefrom.

(4) Curved—forming either a convex or concave arc flaring from the alignment of the abutment breast wall.

The footing of a full abutment height wing wall is usually a continuation of the base portion of the breast wall but may be stepped to a higher or lower elevation to obtain acceptable foundation conditions.

A stub type of straight wing wall is sometimes used in connection with a pier-like or bent-like abutment placed within the end of an embankment. This type, commonly known as "elephant ear" or as "butterfly wing" serves to retain the top portion of the embankment from about the elevation of the bridge seat upward to the roadway elevation. The top surface is battered to conform with the embankment side slope.

Working Stress. See STRESS.